Hangeul

The Korean Alphabet

Hangeul
The Korean Alphabet

Park Chang-won
Translated by Cho Yoon-jung and Han Mi-sun

Ewha Womans University Press

Preface

When anything new comes into existence it must battle for survival with the things that already exist, struggling all its life to expand its scope for survival or activity. Throughout this competition or battle, if it cannot overcome the crises it faces its chances of survival inevitably shrink or disappear altogether. If it does manage to survive, however, it is given the chance to flourish and widely wield its power.

This fundamental principle can also be applied to the history of Hangeul's existence, from the time of its creation to the present.

Hangeul in crisis

The first crisis that Hangeul faced came upon its creation. As a new script, Hangeul was the subject of controversy from the beginning. The ruling elite were used to literary Chinese and had no trouble reading and writing. At a time when the nation paid tribute to the Ming Dynasty (China), they believed creation of a new writing system was a dangerous thing that would deal a decisive blow to written communications in literary Chinese and damage relations with the more powerful nation, and indeed overturn the values of the time. The second crisis came during the reign of Yeonsangun. When an anonymous bill censuring him was written in Hangeul, he commanded that the use and teaching of Hangeul be banned; that those who could read it be prosecuted; that all documents written in

Hangeul be destroyed, and that the author of the bill be found by comparison of Hangeul handwriting examples. The third crisis came with the Japanese occupation of Korea (1910–1945). During the latter half of the period, Japan, having annexed Korea by force, implemented policies of assimilation by wiping out the Korean language (then called "Joseon language") and the people's identity as Koreans. The Japanese imperialists employed measures never seen before anywhere in the world such as brainwashing of another people, banning the use of the mother tongue, and banning the teaching and use of the Korean script.

Overcoming crisis

The objections raised by Choe Man-ri and others were borne down under Hangeul's justification as "a writing system for the ordinary people." When Hangeul was created under the name Hunmin jeongeum, there were opposing views: Choe Man-ri and others who used literary Chinese and sought to maintain values based on Chinese civilization could be called the conservatives, while King Sejong, who sought to promote a new literacy for the people with the creation of a new script, could be called progressive. The victory of progressivism at the time can be chiefly attributed to the king's love for the people. This love for the people is well expressed in the "Yeui" section of the *Hunmin jeongeum* manuscript, which says the king created Hangeul to make the lives of the people easier. The king's will being such, in the end no one could stand against him.

Hangeul's survival despite Yeonsangun's ban on its use was due to the ease with which it could be learnt. As it was so easy to learn and to use, it became a necessary part of education in literary Chinese as well. Chinese character textbooks such as the *Thousand Character Classic* and *Yuhap* were written with instructions in Hangeul. That is, Hangeul was needed in the study of Chinese characters. The famous book *Hunmong jahoe* was also written in such a way that one first had to learn Hangeul to study it. The high efficacy of the script, making it easy to learn and use, promoted the spread of Hangeul among the ordinary people.

The final crisis came in the Japanese occupation period, and this time Hangeul survived thanks to the strong will of the people to protect their culture and identity. Research on Hangeul led by Ju Sigyeong flourished around 1900 when Japan's invasion of Joseon intensified. Hangeul scholars formed an academic society to continue research and organize general rules for the Korean language. Research outcomes include the "Proposal for Unified Korean Orthography," "Inspection of the Standard Language," and "Loanword Orthography," which were immediately translated into educational movements dedicated to preserving the Korean language.

In such circumstances, from October 1942 the Japanese implemented its nation obliteration policy, and this instigated scholars to actively fight to protect the written and spoken Korean language. The past Koreans' love of the nation and their determination to protect it even at the cost of their lives could not be destroyed by any outside influences.

Development of Hangeul in the global context

After Korea's liberation from Japanese rule in 1945, Hangeul began to be introduced to other countries around the world. In 1952, the famous linguist I. J. Gelb, in his book *A Study of Writing*, introduced Hangeul in parentheses along with several African writing systems as a very unique and inscrutable script. But in Geoffrey Sampson's book *Writing Systems* published in 1985, Hangeul is explained in a separate chapter (chapter 7, pp. 120–144) titled "A featural system: Korean Hangul." In the book the author writes, "Hangeul has an intrinsically systematic structure and must be unquestionably ranked as one of the greatest intellectual achievements of mankind."

Following international recognition of the excellence of Hangeul and the achievements of its creator, King Sejong the Great, the UNESCO King Sejong Literary Prize has been awarded since 1990 to reward the activities of individuals or groups working to eradicate illiteracy. In 1997, Hangeul was inscribed on the UNESCO Memory of the World Register. Today Hangeul is a precious treasure not only of the Korean people but of all humanity that must be passed on to the next generation.

Its value recognized around the world, Hangeul is now on the path to globalization. This is evidenced by the expansion of the King Sejong Institute, which is dedicated to the teaching of Korean language and culture. Starting with 13 branches in 3 countries (United States, China, Mongolia) in 2007, it has grown to 120 branches in 52 countries as of December 2013. Branches of the King Sejong Institute are being opened not only in Asia, Europe, America and Oceania but also in Africa. Study of the Korean language in foreign countries has indeed grown. Taking China for example, in the early 1990s when diplomatic relations between Korea and China were normalized, there were only four or five universities in China offering Korean language courses, but this number has grown to over 200 as of 2013.

The Korean language and the Korean script, Hangeul, have survived through many tough moments and are now spreading throughout the world. This book has been written to make the process of Hangeul's development widely known. I would like to thank Ewha Womans University Press for planning this book at an opportune moment, and especially Jeong Gyeong-im, who lent valuable assistance in editing and proofreading of the book.

Park Chang-won

Contents

Hangeul The Korean Alphabet

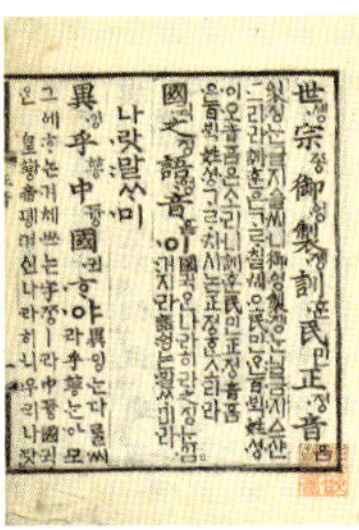
世宗御製訓民正音

I. What is Hangeul?

Human beings have been able to live as lords of all creation due to three major factors. First, human beings are capable of standing on two feet and using their two hands to make tools, which led to the birth of civilization. Second, as they are capable of using fire they can process materials to make different products. Third, they are capable of using language, which enables individual knowledge to be shared with other people. The invention of writing brought radical change to the function of language. When human beings invented language, it transformed the way knowledge and information are stored and shared and led to the development of civilization.

Human writing started with prehistoric pictures and gradually developed from there. In the 15th century, Koreans created Hangeul, which had no connection with any other script. It is the only script in the world that was promulgated with an explanation of the principles behind its creation.

1. A Writing System Invented by Koreans
2. Treasure of Human Culture

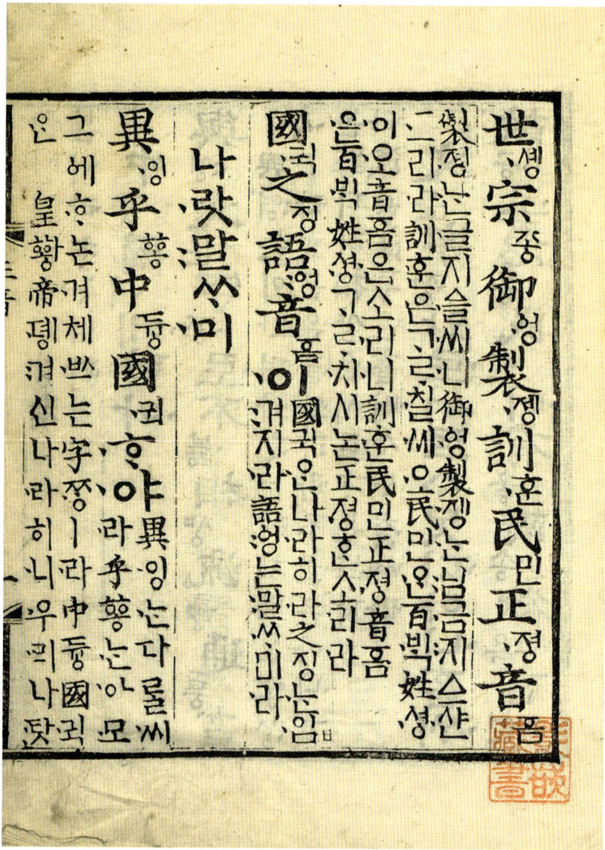

***Hunmin jeongeum* manuscript**, 1568, Woodblock print, Bumwoosa Publishing Co.

1. A Writing System Invented by Koreans

Hangeul is a writing system invented in 1444 by King Sejong, fourth monarch of the Joseon Dynasty (1392–1910). At the time Koreans did not have a writing system that could express the characteristics of their native language and so resorted to the use of Chinese characters to express their intentions or transcribed the Korean language making use of the sounds and meanings of Chinese characters. But as this required Chinese-character literacy, it was largely inaccessible to the general populace. In response to this, King Sejong invented a uniquely Korean script, or writing system, to promote literacy among the ordinary people. The invention of Hangeul is recorded in the *Annals of King Sejong* (*Sejong sillok*) as follows:

> This month the king himself created the 28 letters of Eonmun [Hangeul]. Similar to ancient [Chinese] seal script, the letters are divided into initial sounds, medial sounds, and final sounds and when these sounds are joined together they make syllables. On the whole, it is possible to write down all Chinese sounds and Korean sounds, and while the letters are simple they can be varied infinitely.

This script was originally called Hunmin jeongeum. Today it is called Hangeul.

Explanation of principles and process of creation

After the creation of Hangeul, King Sejong had his ministers write a commentary explaining the script. This book was also called *Hunmin jeongeum*, which literally means "correct sounds to instruct the people," and was promulgated in 1446.

It is largely divided into three parts: "Hunmin jeongeum yeui," which explains the significance of the invention of the new script; "Hunmin jeongeum haerye," which explains the principles behind the script and its usage, and gives examples; and "Jeonginji seomun," an introduction written by Jeong In-ji, which praises the excellence of the new script.

"Hunmin jeongeum haerye" (hereafter the "Haerye") is divided into six parts: an explanation to the principles behind the creation of Hangeul; an explanation of initial sounds; an explanation of medial sounds; an explanation of final sounds; an explanation of the combination of letters; and examples of the letters in use.

Created according to the principles of sound

The creation of Hangeul called for knowledge of the principles of sound, and it is explained in the beginning of the "Haerye" that the principles behind the sounds and the letters are the same.

> In creating the *jeongeum* ["correct sounds"], from the beginning they were not forcibly created anew through research and searching for information but are based on the principles of sound. The principles [of sound and writing] are not two [but one].

Principles of sound derived from observation of the speech organs

In explaining the principles behind the creation of the new script the "Haerye" says: "The 28 correct sounds were made according to the shape of the speech organs." The Hangeul script is composed of the original 28 letters, letters written on top of each other, letters made of double consonants, and letters made of combined consonants. The basic principle behind the creation of all the letters is giving shape to sounds.

An original script

The introduction written by Jeong In-ji states that Hangeul is a completely new script in terms of the fundamental method and principles of creation:

> No reference to old scripts was made in the creation of the correct sounds. They all come from nature.

Here "nature" refers to the laws of nature inherent in heaven and earth. The laws of nature apply to all things in creation and are hence inherent in human sounds as well. Hangeul was made based on those principles of nature.

In regard to the method and principles behind the creation of Hangeul, the introduction mentions the term *jabang gojeon* (字倣古篆) which has had various interpretations, along the lines of "the shape of the letters is similar to the ancient seal script."

In a letter to the king, the scholar Choe Man-ri expressed his own opinions on the term *jabang gojeon* and in the process tried to prove the originality of Hangeul, the basis of his objection to the new script.

Even if it is argued that the Korean script is entirely modeled on old letters and therefore cannot be called new, and that the shapes of the letters are based on seal script, the expression of sound and the method of combining the letters and other features are all opposite to the old ways and hence are not based on an existing script.

2. Treasure of Human Culture

The writing systems used by humankind have evolved over thousands of years from logograms (word representation) to phonemic script. It was millions of years ago that humankind distinguished itself biologically from other living creatures and developed common human characteristics. However, it has not been that long since people began to live in communities and develop culture and civilization. Indeed radical development came only six or seven thousand years ago, when humans developed writing systems and built ancient civilizations. Commonly, the writing used in the four major ancient civilizations of Egypt, Mesopotamia, China and India consisted of hieroglyphics or logograms. Of course, Egyptian hieroglyphics were unique symbols that also had phonetic value, but the writing was fundamentally pictographic.

The Egyptian writing system was transmitted to the Semites, who lived in the Middle East region, the center of civilization at the time, and they developed hieroglyphics to a higher level. By the time it reached the Phoenicians, a branch of the Semites, the system had developed into a phonemic script made up of consonants capable of expressing syllables, and when this was transmitted to the Greeks it developed into a full phonemic script. From there it was transmitted to the Romans and developed into the Roman alphabet, which is

Fragments of tortoiseshell and bone, National Museum of Korea used in Western Europe, America, Australia and other parts of the world today. Separately, it was also transmitted to the Slav people and developed into the Cyrillic script, which was also passed on to the nations of the former Soviet Union area.

In the ancient Qin Dynasty, writing was unified in China under Qin Shi Huang, the first emperor, and various styles of script were developed for the Chinese language. Chinese characters were modified as they spread to nearby peoples, resulting in the Khitan script and the Jurchen script. When they reached Japan they formed the base of the Japanese syllabic script and in Korea they were used to express Korean in modified forms called Idu and Gugyeol.

A script that changed the history of writing

In the 15th century, when Hangeul was invented, various writing systems were in use around the world: Chinese characters, which are both ideographs and logograms at the same time; the Japanese syllabic script derived from Chinese characters; the Roman and Cyrillic alphabets, which are both phonograms and phonemic script; the Tibetan and Mongol scripts, which are phonemic scripts derived from the Semitic script; and phonemic scripts developed in India and Southeast Asia. What is common to all the writing systems of these ancient civilizations, including Egypt, Mesopotamia, India and China, is that they are all based in logograms – in other words, their scripts are based on symbols that express words or morphemes.

Among these ancient scripts, the Mesopotamian and Indian scripts faded out of existence while Chinese characters were transmitted to nearby countries, where they came to be used in modified forms. In China, however, they remain in use as logograms. The Egyptian script was transformed into a syllabic script when it was transmitted to the Semites. This was then transmitted to the Greeks via the Phoenicians, a branch of the Semites, and was turned into a phonemic script three thousand years ago. This script was then transmitted to the Romans and Slavic peoples and spread to the world where they are still in use today.

Following on from this, the Hunmin jeongeum (Hangeul) was created in the Joseon Dynasty, some six hundred years ago. As the letters were devised based on observation of the shapes and features of the speech organs, Hangeul is considered a "featural writing system" in which the elements that make up the phonemes, such as voicing or place of articulation, are reflected in the shape of the letters. In this sense, the creation of Hangeul changed the history of writing systems used by humanity, shifting the course of script development from "logographic system→syllabic system→phonemic system" to "logographic system→syllabic system→phonemic system→featural system."

The term "featural writing system" was coined by the world famous linguist Geoffrey Sampson to describe Hangeul as a script where the phonetic value of a letter is indicated by the form of the letter. In 1989 UNESCO instituted an award for people and institutions working to eradicate illiteracy, and that award is named the King Sejong Literacy Prize. Then in 1997, the *Hunmin jeongeum* manuscript was inscribed on the UNESCO Memory of the World Register, a list of significant and valuable documentary heritage.

The only script in the world with known creator, principles, and time of invention

Of the some 400 writing systems in the world, Hangeul is the only one whose creators, principles and time of invention are known. The book titled *Hunmin jeongeum* is the only one in the world to explain the objectives and principles behind the creation of a writing system. Many records do exist as to the origins or creators of other writing systems – for example, they will say who directed whom to develop a script and when – but *Hunmin jeongeum* is the only book that explains the objectives of creating the script, the principles and the whole process of its development.

Vowels in dots and lines, consonants in squares, circles and triangles

The vowels of Hangeul consist of lines (vertical and horizontal) and dots. These elements are combined in a way that is parallel to their phonetic values. For example, the vowels that are "lying down" (horizontal base: ㅗ, ㅜ, ㅚ, ㅟ) are rounded sounds (made with rounded lips) while the ones that are "standing up" (vertical base: ㅓ, ㅏ, ㅔ, ㅐ) are flat sounds (made with a straight mouth). If the vowel contains two dots (ㅕ, ㅑ, ㅛ, ㅠ) these become double vowels with ascending sounds and if the vowel has a vertical line at the end (ㅚ, ㅟ, ㅔ, ㅐ) these are double vowels with descending sounds. When a consonant maintains a consistent shape, the place of articulation is always the same. Complex letters made up of many strokes have a stronger sound, while the simpler ones have a softer sound. So with knowledge of the type of letter and type of sound, the phonetic value of any letter can be guessed from its shape. (refer to pp. 56–63)

Ⅱ. Creation of the Hunmin jeongeum

In January 1444, King Sejong personally invented a new writing system and named it "Hunmin jeongeum," which means "correct sounds to instruct the people." In the process of laying the foundations for rule of a new nation, Sejong believed that it was important for the ordinary people to be able to read and write. To make this possible, he applied the principles of all things in the universe to sounds and letters, and this led to the creation of a new script.

The *Hunmin jeongeum* manuscript is composed of three parts: "*Hunmin jeongeum yeui*," which explains the significance of the invention of the new script; "*Hunmin jeongeum haerye*," which explains the principles behind the script and its usage, and gives examples; and "*Jeonginji seomun*," an introduction written by Jeong In-ji, which praises the excellence of the new script.

1. Background to the Creation of Hangeul
2. King Sejong, Creator of Hangeul
3. Composition and Content of the *Hunmin jeongeum* Manuscript

Inner Placenta Jar and Stone Tablet from the Placenta Chamber of King Sejong.
National Palace Museum of Korea

1. Background to the Creation of Hangeul

King Sejong is considered to be the greatest monarch in Korean history, the king with the greatest abilities and most notable achievements. But his greatness was rooted not only in his abilities and the historical context of the Joseon Dynasty, but also in his love for the people. King Sejong championed many policies and systems, published books in various fields, and implemented strategies designed to protect the country from foreign invasion–all because of his love for the people and his desire to protect them and ensure a stable livelihood for them. If we were to choose the single achievement of King Sejong that ensured his place in history, it would have to be the creation of Hunmin jeongeum, or Hangeul. This too was motivated by his love for the people.

> Even a person with good reason can only judge the seriousness of a crime based on the laws, so how can the foolish common people judge the size of their crime and fix their ways on their own? Although it is not possible to teach all the common people the laws, how would it be if we were to select and write down the major crimes and have them translated into Idu and distribute them to the people, hence helping all unlearned men and women to avoid crime?

It was King Sejong's perception of the plight of ordinary people that drove him to create a new script. This motivation is explained in "Hunmin jeongeum yeui":

1. As the sounds of Korean words are different to those of Chinese words, it is difficult for Koreans to communicate with each other using Chinese characters.
2. Although the ordinary people have things they want to say, many of them cannot express what they want to say in writing.
3. Taking pity on the people, I [Sejong] have made 28 letters that all people can easily learn and use in their everyday lives.

This consciousness led King Sejong to create one of the most brilliant writing systems in the world. Until that time, Koreans had been borrowing[1] Chinese characters to express their native language. Borrowing the logographic system of another country and using it as a phonemic system proved very unsatisfactory, however, and Chinese characters did not work well as a means for transcribing the Korean language.

This reality, knowledge of the writing systems used by neighboring countries (for example, the Mongols were using a phonemic script by modifying the scripts of others), and knowledge of phonetics and rhyme dictionaries, led to the birth of the "featural" writing system[2] Hunmin jeongeum in the 15th century.

1. Borrowing the writing of another country to write down a nation's language is called *chaja*.
2. A type of phonographic script, a featural writing system reflects phonemic features such as place of articulation in the shape of the letters.

Borrowing the sounds and meanings of Chinese characters to express proper nouns

As Koreans previously had no script of their own, they learnt the Chinese characters used in the region, and when writing used literary Chinese or modified Chinese characters to transcribe Korean. They did this by borrowing either the meaning or the pronunciation of Chinese characters, and in the early days it appears that both methods were used together.

When writing down the name of King Hyeokgeose, founder of the Silla Kingdom, it is recorded in Vol.1 of *History of the Three Kingdoms (Samguk sagi)* that the name "Hyeokgeose" is a transcribed version of "Gwangmyeongise," which means "ruling the world with light." It was a name that made use of the character *hyeok* (赫), which means "bright" or "radiant." When it comes to geographic names, both the sound and meaning of Chinese characters were borrowed. For example, the city of Suwon, originally called Maehol, was written as both Maehol (買忽) and Suseong (水城). Maehol, pronounced Maihu in Chinese, uses characters that try to represent the sounds of the name, while Suseong, meaning "water city," uses characters that represent the meaning of the name.

Inconvenience of using Chinese characters

In Chinese, one character is pronounced as one syllable and this becomes one morpheme.[3] But in Korean, there are many cases where the morpheme is composed of more than one syllable. For this rea-

3. The smallest grammatical unit in a language that contains meaning

son the number of borrowed characters does not match the number of morphemes in Korean. Moreover, as each Chinese character has various meanings, it was difficult to choose which one to adopt in each case. Therefore, various ways were explored to achieve expression closer to the actual Korean with the use of borrowed characters, and in this process several distinctive traits emerged.

For example, when writing down one word it became more and more common to place the part conveying meaning at the front and the part conveying sound at the back. Meaning was conveyed more clearly by reinforcing grammatical morphemes and making sentences that were more distinctly Korean.

Such efforts resulted in greater accuracy in writing Korean with borrowed characters and this developed in two directions. On one hand, various Chinese-character morphemes were borrowed to transcribe the Korean language, and on the other Chinese characters were used along with grammatical morphemes or markers. The former system is called Hyangchal and the latter Idu.

Hyangchal

Following is an example of *hyangga* (an ancient form of poetic song) written in Hyangchal, from "Jemangmae-ga," or "Requiem for a Dead Sister."

一等隱枝良出古 去奴隱處毛冬乎丁.
ᄒᆞᄃᆞᆫ 가지라 나고 가논 곳 모ᄃᆞᆯ온뎌.

Though [the leaves are] from the same branch
They know net where they go.

Comparing the original with the Korean interpretation, the Chinese characters used in the original represent a mixture of meanings (called *hun*) and sound (called *eum*). Specifically, the character types are in the order of meaning+sound+sound, meaning+sound, meaning+sound, meaning+sound+sound, meaning, sound+sound+sound+sound. Though the given example is only part of the poem, it can be seen that the meaning elements tend to be placed at the front and the sound elements at the back. This was a fairly typical pattern for poems written in Hyangchal. The characters representing sound such as 等 and 隱 represent morphemes or end markers, and those that are independent morphemes such as 良 and 古 are used to represent particles or verb endings.

As shown in the above example, Chinese characters were used for their meaning or sound to represent single-syllable morphemes or final-consonant sounds of morphemes in the native Korean language. This means Chinese characters, part of a logographic script, were used in the manner of a syllabic script[4] or phonemic script,[5] which is a rather radical adaptation.

Idu

Hyangchal was generally used to write poetry while Idu was used to write prose. The two systems are essentially the same however, except that in Idu the original sound and meaning of Chinese characters are used as full morphemes.[6] Following is a simple example of

4. A phonographic script where one syllable is one character that cannot be further divided, for example Japanese *kana*
5. A phonographic script where the sounds are expressed in phonemic units, for example Hangeul, the Roman alphabet, etc.
6. A morpheme that expresses a concrete object, movement or state

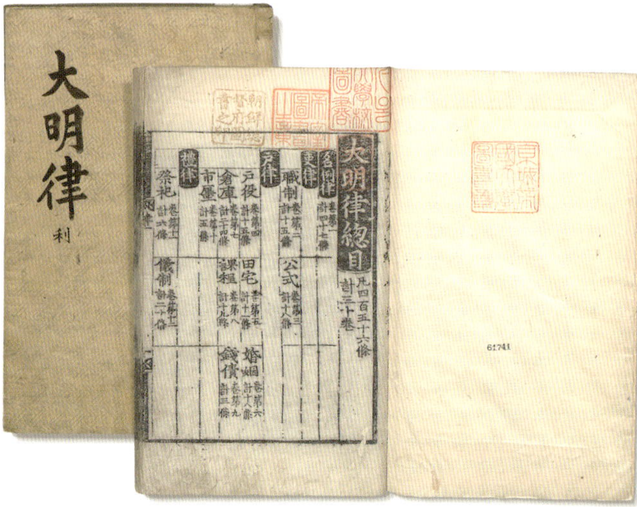

Idu translation of the *Daminglu* (*Great Ming Code*). Kyujanggak Institute for Korean Studies

Idu from *Yangjam gyeongheom chwalyo*, a book on sericulture.

> 蠶段 陽物是乎等用良 水氣乙 厭却 桑葉叱分 喫破爲遣 飮水不冬.
> 蠶ᄯᆞᆫ陽物이온ᄃᆞᆯ쓰아 水氣ᄅᆞᆯ厭却 桑葉ᄲᅮᆫ喫破ᄒᆞ고 飮水안ᄃᆞᆯ.

As silkworms are creatures with strong yang energy, they do not like water. They only eat mulberry leaves and do not drink water.

The final consonant additions found in Hyangchal are rarely seen in Idu, the reason being that in the transcription of full morphemes the original meaning and sound of the Chinese characters is used. In writing down grammatical morphemes, Chinese characters are used in the manner of syllabic script. Given these factors it can be said that Idu is also a radical innovation.

Gugyeol

Gugyeol is essentially a system of rendering texts written in Chinese into understandable Korean with the use of explanatory markers in Hangeul or Chinese characters. Seokdok Gugyeol refers to unmodified Chinese-character texts featuring these markers (called *to*) inserted to the left or right of phrases to enable the Chinese characters to be read as Korean. In other words, it was effectively a method of translation. The following is the first sentence of the *Earlier Translation of the Humane King Sutra (Guyeok inwanggyeong)* written in Gugyeol:

信行乚 具足ソニ㢱 復ソㄱ 有セナ㢱 五道セ 一切衆生リ 、
復ソㄱ 有セナ㢱 他方セ 不矢リヒセ 可セソㄱ· 量ノホ、衆、

The original text was arranged vertically but here it is arranged horizontally for editing purposes. The Gugyeol markers on the left were written down as superscript and those on the right as subscript. If rewritten according to the way in which the sentence is read, the sentence is as follows:[7]

信行乚 具足ソニ㢱 復ソㄱ 五道セ 一切 衆生リ 有セナ㢱 復ソㄱ 他
方セ 量ノホ 可セソㄱ 不矢リヒセ 衆 有セナ㢱

7. The sentence was written in Chinese word order but read in Korean word order according to the instructions provided by the markers.

Some 70 Gugyeol characters were used altogether. They mostly indicated grammatical morphemes such as particles, verb stems and verbal suffixes and were created by simplifying Chinese characters through the reduction of strokes. That is, a logographic script was modified to transcribe syllables, which is why the characters were divided into different levels. Likewise, Gugyeol was a true innovation.

Inadequacy of using borrowed Chinese characters

The basic knowledge that enabled creation of the Humin jeongeum (Hangeul) was the perception that uttered sounds could be categorized as initial, medial, and final sounds. This idea is reflected in earlier Korean scripts that made use of borrowed Chinese characters. From the Three Kingdoms period, when Chinese characters were first borrowed to write down Korean, various methods were devised for doing so. But differences in the Chinese and Korean phoneme systems made it impossible to transcribe the Korean phonemes that did not exist in Chinese. Therefore, the Korean phoneme system could not be accurately reflected, which created challenges for written communication.

For example, the ancient Korean phoneme · had no equivalent Chinese phoneme and could not be expressed in Chinese, thus resulting in confusion in expressing this in written form. Further, the syllabic composition of Korean, that is, the combination of initial consonant and medial vowel, or the combination of medial vowel and final consonant, was different to Chinese and therefore could not be properly expressed with borrowed Chinese characters.

In addition, the grammatical morphemes, which exist in Korean but not in Chinese, were expressed in various ways such as sound-borrowed characters (*eumcha*),[8] meaning-borrowed characters (*hun-cha*),[9] reading for sound value (*eumdok*),[10] and reading for meaning (*hundok*).[11] But the challenges were significant. Recognition of this problem is reflected in the introduction to the *Hunmin jeongeum* written by Jeong In-ji:

> Most foreign languages [aside from Chinese] have their own sounds, but as they have no script with which to write down the sounds they borrow Chinese characters for this purpose. But like a square stick in a round hole, they do not work well together. How is it possible to master it easily or read it fluently!

> In the old days, the great scholar Seol Chong of Silla developed Idu and this is still in use today in government and among the common people. But as this requires the borrowing of Chinese characters it is very rough and sometimes comes to a dead end, and is very coarse and inconsistent. In the expression of [our] language, it does not even fulfill one ten thousandth [of our needs].

As this shows, Koreans had a script but not one of their own. Although the Koreans adapted Chinese characters for their use it was not actually suitable for transcribing Korean. So in order to properly transcribe the native language the need arose for the creation of a new script.

8. Borrowing the sound of Chinese characters to express Korean
9. Borrowing the meaning of Chinese characters to express Korean
10. Reading Chinese characters for their sound value
11. Reading Chinese characters for their meaning

Chinese yunxue and the writing of neighboring countries

Chinese yunxue (traditional study of rhymes) and Neo-Confucianism

When King Sejong was ruler of the Joseon Dynasty, in China the Ming Dynasty was rising in power after the collapse of the Yuan Dynasty. Rhyme books published by the Yuan Dynasty include *Rhymes of the Central Plains (Zhongyuan yinyun)*, completed in 1324, *Ancient and Modern Rhymes (Gujin yunhui)*, and *Abridged Version of Collection of Rhymes from Ancient to Modern Times (Gujin yunhui juyao)*. Another from the early Ming Dynasty is *Hongwu zhengyun*, completed in 1375. These books show great variation in content. In accordance with the changes in China's political situation, King Sejong felt the need to reorganize the use of Chinese-character sounds in Korea, the result of which was the rhyme book *Standard Rhymes of the Eastern State (Dongguk jeongun)*, published in 1447 and distributed in 1448.

Before publication of *Standard Rhymes of the Eastern State*, King Sejong commissioned the translation of Chinese rhyme books and sent scholar-officials such as Sin Suk-ju and Seong Sam-mun to Huang Zan in Liadong, to research original rhyme books of China. As the new script Hunmin jeongeum had already been created by this time, these endeavors were ultimately aimed at creating a book explaining the new script and organizing the script in a more systematic fashion according to the principles of Neo-Confucianism.

It is assumed that prior to the creation of Hangeul, Sejong would have already studied a variety of rhyme books published in China. Those that likely had the greatest influence on Hangeul are the rhyme dictionaries *Qieyun* (literally "cut rhymes"),[12] *Guangyun* ("broad rhymes")[13] from the Sui and Tang dynasties, and the rhyme

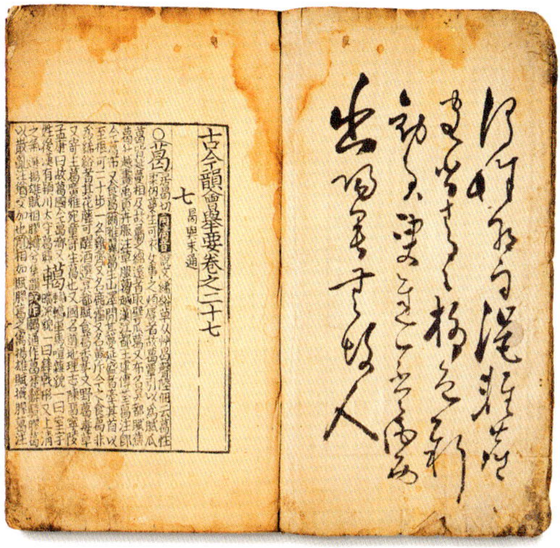

Gujin yunhui juyao (Abridged Version of Collection of Rhymes from Ancient to Modern Times), 1434, National Museum of Korea

tables "Dengyuntu," ("diagram of classified rhymes"), which categorize Chinese syllables according to the way they are read. These are phonological tables with the sounds of Chinese words arranged in vertical and horizontal columns for easy analysis.

The tables were concerned with systematic classification of the initial consonants in a syllable (*shengmu*),[14] medial-final combined consonants (*yunmun*),[15] and tones (*shengdiao*), and this had a direct impact on the creation of the Hunmin jeongeum. The greatest influence came from the description of initial consonants. That is, they

12. A rhyme dictionary published in 601 (Sui Dynasty), written by Lu Fayan
13. A rhyme dictionary published in the Song Dynasty
14. The first part of a Chinese syllable, equivalent to the initial sound in Korean
15. The last part of a Chinese syllable

were described as velar, alveolar, bilabial, dental, and glottal sounds, which distinguish the place of articulation of sounds, and the classification of methods of articulation as either voiced or unvoiced sounds, were both applied intact in the creation of the Hunmin jeongeum.

The writing of neighboring countries

In the 15th century, Manchuria was home to various peoples including the Mongols, the Manchurians, the Khitans, and the Jurchens. That the writing systems used by them served as a motive or background to the creation of the Hunmin jeongeum is mentioned in *Bohanje jip*, a collection of writings by Sin Suk-ju.

> Although Korean phonemes are different to those of Chinese, the velar, alveolar, bilabial, dental and glottal sounds [position of the consonants], as are the voiced and unvoiced sounds [method of articulation], the pitch [rhythmic elements of the sounds] and other elements are no different to the sounds of Chinese. All countries have writing systems to suit their own respective languages and are using them to express their national languages. As we are the only country without our own script, the king has created 28 Eonmun [Hangeul] letters.

The scripts used by neighboring countries at the time are as follows:

Mongolian script: When Genghis Khan unified the Yuan Empire, in order to address the inconvenience of having no writing system he created the Mongolian script based on the Uighur script. This script is the basis for the modern Mongolian alphabet.

Phags-pa script: The Phags-pa script was created by reinforcing the weaknesses of the script used by the Mongols before establishment

Bronze Mirror with Inscription in Khitan Script. Goryeo Dynasty. National Museum of Korea of the Yuan Empire. Based on the Tibetan script, which belongs to the Sanskrit family, it was created by the Tibetan monk Phags-pa in 1269 as a phonemic script written in syllabic blocks.

Khitan large script: After founding the Liao Dynasty, in the early 10th century the Khitans adapted Chinese characters to create some 3,000 "large characters," which are known as the Khitan large script.

Khitan small script: This is a phonographic writing system based on the Uighur script. In the early 12th century, the Jurchens, after founding the Jin Dynasty, created their own phonographic script based on the Khitan small script.

Tibetan script: A minister of Tibet was sent to India to study the grammar and phonetics of the grammarian Panini and upon his return to Tibet created a phonographic script for transcribing the Tibetan language. This alphabet is still in use in Tibet today.

Accumulation of phonological knowledge

Three-part division of syllables and discovery of phonetic features

The basic unit of human speech is the syllable. Although the syllable may be comprised of a single vowel, generally it is made up of an initial consonant, a medial vowel, and a final consonant. Through careful observation, the creator of the Hunmin jeongeum divided each syllable into these three parts. Though realizing that the same consonant had a different sound depending on whether it was in first or final position in the syllable, Sejong ignored the phonetic differentiation according to the position differentiation and used the same letter for both sounds according to the phonemic representation. In the study of the phonology of Chinese, which is a language isolate, the syllables are separated into two parts in order to indicate rhyme. But Korean is an agglutinative language where different elements are added to the root, thus bringing much change to the sound of the initial and final consonants. Observing this, Sejong created the initial and final sounds in the same form.

It is likely that Sejong had gained the idea for such division of syllables into three parts from the method of transcription used for borrowed Chinese characters that had been used up to that time. That is, with borrowed characters, sometimes only the medial vowel was written down, sometimes only the final consonant, and sometimes the initial and final consonant. From this system of transcription Sejong was familiar with the division of syllables.

The definitive reason why the letters of Hangeul are so systematic and well-structured is that certain qualities inherent in the phonemes were recognized and reflected in the creation of the script. The acoustic qualities arising from the method of articulation of the consonants were divided into *cheong* and *tak*, or "clear" and "muddy." These categories were again subdivided into wholly clear, partly clear, wholly muddy, and neither clear nor muddy. The strongest sounds were the partly clear ones, the most complicated sounds of their types (ㅋ, ㅌ, ㅍ, ㅊ, ㅎ). Because the wholly muddy consonants become thick, they were combined with the wholly clear ones (ㄲ, ㄸ, ㅃ, ㅆ, ㅉ, excepting ㆅ).

The features of the vowels were divided according the position of the tongue and shape of the mouth in their articulation. The feature related to the tongue is *chuk* (retraction), which was subdivided into non-retraction, small retraction, and retraction, the basic letters being ㅣ, ㅡ and ㆍ respectively. The features related to the mouth were divided into *gucheok* (mouth closed) and *gujang* (mouth open). *Gucheok* was subdivided so that the featureless vowels are the basic vowels and those with features are formed by placing ㆍ over or under ㅡ. Hence the letters constituting the rounded vowels appear to be "lying down." Vowels corresponding to the *gujang* feature are formed by placing · to the front or back (left or right) of ㅣ. Hence the letters constituting the unrounded vowels appear to be "standing up."

Observation of method and place of articulation of consonants

King Sejong observed the shape and movement of the mouth and lips when speaking. According to the point of articulation where the active (moving) and passive (stationary) articulators meet, the consonants were classified as velar sounds (back of the tongue), alveolar sounds (tip of the tongue), bilabial sounds (lips), dental sounds (teeth), and glottal sounds (throat). Also, according to the mode of articulation, sounds were classified as either "clear" or "muddy." The simple consonants ㄱ, ㄷ, ㅂ, ㅅ, ㅈ are wholly clear, the aspirated consonants ㅋ, ㅌ, ㅍ, ㅊ are partly clear, the fortis consonants ㄲ, ㄸ, ㅃ, ㅆ, ㅉ are wholly muddy, and the remaining consonants ㄴ, ㅁ, ㆁ, ㄹ, ㅿ are neither clear nor muddy.

That is, the consonants were classified according to place and method of articulation, and these characteristics were reflected in the design of the letters.

Observation of vowel articulation

The vowels are divided into single and double vowels. The single vowels are articulated by the lips and the tongue. In articulation, the lips are either rounded (rounded vowel) or straight (unrounded vowel). The action of the tongue is divided into two basic types: the tongue moves forward toward the lips or retracts to the back of the mouth, and the vowels are divided into front vowels and non-front vowels, or front vowels, central vowels and back vowels. In addition, vowels that are articulated with the lips slightly parted and the tongue almost touching the roof of the mouth are called high vowels, with the lips slightly parted and the tongue in central position are called mid vowels, and with the mouth wide open and the tongue in the lowest position are called low vowels. When classified not according to the position of the tongue but the extent to which the mouth is opened the vowels are called open vowels, middle vowels and closed vowels respectively.

In regard to the shape of the mouth and position of the tongue when articulating vowels, King Sejong wrote the following:

> As the tongue is retracted the sound is deep, and is equated with the heavens opening at the *ja* hour [between 11 p.m. and 1 a.m.]. So the vowel ㆍ was created first. The round shape is modeled on heaven.
>
> As the tongue is slightly retracted the sound is neither deep nor shallow, and is equated with the earth opening at the *chuk* hour [between 1 a.m. and 3 a.m.]. So the vowel ㅡ was created second. The flatness of the shape is modeled on the earth.
>
> As the tongue is not retracted the sound is shallow, and is equated with the appearance of man at the *in* hour [between 3 a.m. and 5 a.m.]. So the vowel ㅣ was created third. The shape is modeled on the form of a person standing upright.

In regard to the shape of the mouth, King Sejong wrote as follows:

> ㅗ is the same type of vowel as ㆍ. It is made with the mouth narrowed, the letter ㆍ harmonizing with ㅡ to form the shape of heaven and earth uniting for the first time.
>
> ㅜ is the same type of vowel as ㅡ. It is made with the mouth narrowed, the letter ㅡ harmonizing with ㆍ to form the shape of heaven and earth uniting for the first time.
>
> ㅏ is the same type of vowel as ㆍ. It is made with the mouth open,

the letter ㅣ harmonizing with · to form the shape of heaven and earth, whose action is reflected in all things, waiting for completion in man.

ㅓ is the same type of vowel as ㅡ. It is made with the mouth open, the letter · harmonizing with ㅣ to form the shape of heaven and earth, whose action is reflected in all things, waiting for completion in man.

Finally, in regard to the double vowels, King Sejong wrote as follows:

ㅛ is the same as ㅗ but originates from ㅣ
ㅑ is the same as ㅏ but originates from ㅣ
ㅠ is the same as ㅜ but originates from ㅣ
ㅕ is the same as ㅓ but originates from ㅣ

Observation of proportional relationship between sounds

King Sejong noted that sounds do not exist in isolation but in relationship with other sounds and also reflected this in the design of the letters. In the case of consonants, he perceived that the strengths of the sounds were proportionately related according to the method of articulation – wholly clear: partly clear: wholly muddy: neither clear nor muddy. Such relationship[16] between sounds was reflected in the shapes of the letters.

In the table on the facing page, although there is some difference according to the characteristics of each consonant, the stronger partly clear sounds were created by adding a stroke to the wholly clear sounds. The wholly muddy sounds are made by doubling the wholly clear sounds, thus reflecting the proportional strength of the

16. According to the Russian linguist Nikolai Sergeevich Trubetskoi, these sounds are in a proportional relationship.

	Neither clear nor muddy	Wholly clear	Partly clear	Wholly muddy
Velar	(ㅇ)	ㄱ	ㅋ	ㄲ
Alveolar	ㄴ	ㄷ	ㅌ	ㄸ
Bilabial	ㅁ	ㅂ	ㅍ	ㅃ
Dental	ㅿ	ㅅ		ㅆ
		ㅈ	ㅊ	ㅊ
Glottal	ㅇ	ㆆ	ㅎ	ㆅ

sounds in the form of the letters.

In the case of the vowels, through observation of the movement and shape of the lips and tongue when voicing the sounds, King Sejong realized that there was a proportional relationship between them and reflected this fact in the design of the letters.

Portrait of King Sejong, King Sejong Memorial Society

2. King Sejong, Creator of Hangeul

Who is King Sejong?

King Sejong was the fourth monarch of the Joseon Dynasty. Although the third son of King Taejong, he was chosen as crown prince for his love of learning and his fine personal character. He rose to the throne at the age of 22. Often called the "sage king" or King Sejong the Great, he was born in 1397, became king in 1418, and remained on the throne until 1450. He served as a model for those who came behind him and is still revered as the greatest king in Korean history. During his reign, his achievements included establishing the Confucian culture and promoting a flourishing folk culture. But his greatest achievement was the creation of the Hunmin jeongeum (Hangeul), which left a great mark in the world history of writing systems.

It is said King Sejong was a voracious reader from childhood. He read and reread not only the classics of Confucianism, the ruling ideology of the time, but also books across a wide range of fields including law, history, astronomy, music and medicine. It appears that he read so much that he worried his father, King Taejong, who is recorded as saying, "Even when it is very cold or very hot, he reads through the night. For fear of him falling ill, I forbade him to read at night, but he just asked for all of my thickest books and took them away."

This love of learning is the spirit that drove King Sejong to reform areas such as institutions, learning and the arts. In 1420, the second year of his reign, inside the palace he established Jiphyeonjeon (Hall of Worthies), a kind of research institute, where he cultivated scholars who would revere learning and provide a supporting role for his rule. Authoring books in varied fields including history, geography, politics, economics, astronomy, ethics, propriety, literature, rhyme, religion, military affairs, agriculture, medicine and music, King Sejong laid the foundations for the culture and civilization of the Joseon Dynasty.

Achievements of King Sejong

Development of new type printing and publishing techniques

In 1420, King Sejong led the development of a new font called Gyeongja, but as the characters were thin and tightly spaced, they were difficult to read. So in 1434 (16th year of his reign), the Gabin year, he ordered the development of a new font. The finest scientists and technicians responsible for making astronomical instruments such as Yi Cheon, Kim Don, Kim Bin, Jang Yeong-sil, Yi Se-hyeong, Jeong Cheok, and Yi Sun-ji, took part in the project. Over two months they managed to make some 20,000 characters, which came to be called the Gabin font. Famed for its beauty, the new typeface played an instrumental role in the development of printing in the Joseon Dynasty. It was the first typeface to be used in the printing of Hangeul.

Development of astronomical instruments for daily life

In 1433, King Sejong invented an armillary sphere for astronomical observation and a water clock, and the following year he invented a sundial. Then in 1441 he invented a rain gauge called Cheugugi and a water gauge (pluviometer) called Supyo, used to measure the water level in rivers. In the same year, he also published a book on astronomy. The rain gauge was the world's first, predating by some 200 years the rain gauge invented by the Italian Benedetto Castelli in 1639.

Reform and reorganization of systems for the people

By reorganizing the system of weights and measures, King Sejong helped to increase transparency in economic activity and prepared standards for economic policies. He compiled the book *Straight Talk on Farming (Nongsa jikseol)*, which contributed to the development of agriculture, and also reformed the taxation system. Moreover, he reorganized medical institutions and compiled books that brought advances to the medical field. These books include *Monthly Ordinances of Collecting Medical Plants (Hyangyak chaechwi wollyeong)*, *Compilation of Native Korean Prescriptions (Hyangyak jipseongbang)*, and *Uibang ryuchwi*, a medical encyclopedia. For the comfort of prisoners King Sejong also improved prison conditions, and to prevent people from being unjustly accused of crime, he instituted the Sambok law, a system enabling up to three appeals.

For the protection of children and the elderly, Sejong forbade the imprisonment of children under the age of 15 or old people over the age of 70 for any crimes less than murder or robbery. Even in the case of crimes worthy of execution, he forbade imprisonment of children under the age of 10 and the elderly over the age of 80. Moreover, Sejong frequently granted criminals amnesty and gave them the opportunity to rejoin society, and by improving conditions for bonded servants (called *nobi*), he enabled them to lead more decent human lives. Aside from these examples, King Sejong implemented many policies and reformed other systems and institutions to improve the lives of the ordinary people.

Reorganization of music and customs

At the command of King Sejong, Park Yeon put in order the music performed in the court and among the general public, rearranging some works and making new instruments. *Musical Scores of King Sejong (Sejong akbo)*, comprising Vols. 136–137 and 140–147 of the *Annals of King Sejong (Sejong sillok)*, brings together all the musical rearrangements and newly created works from this time. This collection divides music into *a-ak* (classical court music) and *sin-ak* (new music). It is the oldest book of musical scores produced in Korea and the first to use mensural notation.[17] At the same time it is the oldest musical score in Asia to be written in mensural notation.

Record of Filial Piety (Hyohaengnok), which came out in the Goryeo Dynasty, promotes the virtue of respect for ons's parents and elders. King Sejong had Seol Sun and others revise the contents and republished the book in 1428. He also had *Illustrated Guide to the Three Bonds (Samgang haengsildo)* published in 1434. The three bonds (of Confucianism) refer to the relationships between subject and ruler, father and son, and husband and wife. The book introduces the deeds of 105 people, 35 case studies each of exemplary loyal subjects, filial children, and faithful wives.

17. A form of notation that reflects the pitch and length of a note

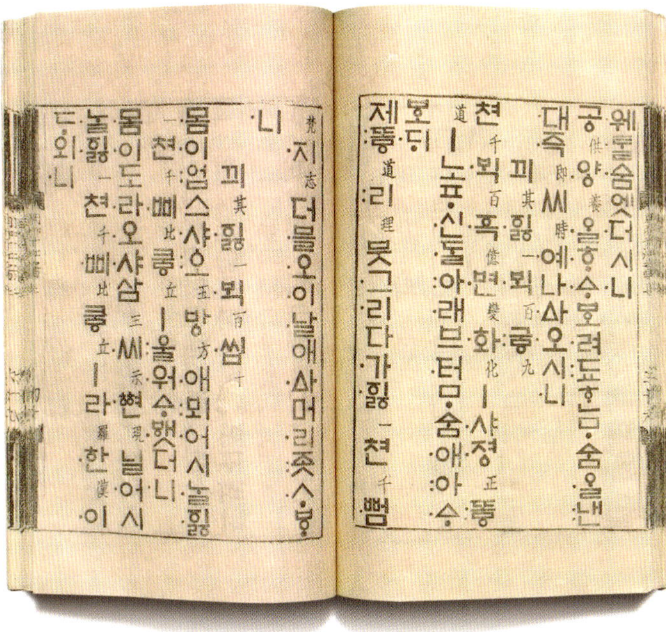

***Songs of the Moon's Reflection on a Thousand Rivers (Wolin cheongang jigok)*.**
Treasure No. 398, Mirae-N

Hemispheric Sundial (Angbui Igu), Treasure No. 845, National Palace Museum of Korea

Rain Gauge Stand, National Palace Museum of Korea

Raising historical awareness

To promote historical awareness in the monarchs of future generations, King Sejong organized the compilation of several history books such as *History of Goryeo (Goryeosa)*, and books that would teach the people about the rises and falls of the nation, including *Mirror on Self-governing Principles (Jachi tonggam hunui)* and *Exemplar for Efficient Government (Chipyeong yoram)*. In 1450 (32nd year of his reign), he had Jeong In-ji, Yu Hyo-tong, and Yi Seok-hyeong compile books on war strategy that contained a history of wars the nation had fought along with comments made by Confucian scholars of the past, as a way to urge kings of future generations to prepare for war.

Moreover, King Sejong also commissioned the epic poem *Songs of the Flying Dragons (Yongbi eocheonga)*, which was the first piece of literature to be written in Hangeul. The poem celebrates the achievements of former kings and serves as justification for the foundation of the Joseon Dynasty and as a reminder for future kings of times when the king brought the country to ruin.

Development of arms and territorial expansion

Modifying the fire arrows and guns developed during the preceding Goryeo Dynasty, King Sejong brought unprecedented innovation to the development of arms in Korea and, with his conquest of regions in the north and south, expanded the national territory. In 1419, acting under the king's command, Yi Jong-mu conquered the island of Daemado. In 1433, the king commanded Choe Yun-deok to suppress the people living in the northwest (now Pyeonganbuk-do Province, North Korea) and set up four military forts on the northern border. The following year, he sent General Kim Jong-seo to suppress the Jurchens living in the northeast border area (now Hamgyeongbuk-do Province, North Korea) and established six

Conquest of Li Manzhu, Jurchen Chieftan, King Sejong Memorial Society posts. Joseon territory was hence expanded northward to the Yalu and Tumen rivers.

Creation of the Hunmin jeongeum

Among the many achievements of King Sejong as mentioned above, it can be argued that his greatest achievement was the invention of the Korean script, originally named Hunmin jeongeum and today called Hangeul. The creation of any writing system is a significant event in the progress of a civilization. King Sejong is the first individual, however, to be credited with creating a completely new script. Through the creation of the Hunmin jeongeum, King Sejong remains one of the greatest figures in Korean history and an eternal light for the Korean people.

3. Composition and Content of the *Hunmin jeongeum* Manuscript

As mentioned above, the book *Hunmin jeongeum* is composed of three parts: "Hunmin jeongeum yeui," which explains the significance of the invention of the new script; "Hunmin jeongeum haerye," which explains the principles behind the script and its usage, and gives examples; and "Jeonginji seomun," an introduction written by Jeong In-ji, which praises the excellence of the new script.

"Hunmin jeongeum haerye" is divided into six parts: an explanation to the principles behind the design of the new script ("Jejahae"); an explanation of initial sounds ("Choseonghae"); an explanation of medial sounds ("Jungseonghae"); an explanation of final sounds ("Jongseonghae"); an explanation of the combination of letters ("Hapjahae"); and examples of the letters in use ("Yongjarye"), with 94 native Korean words written in the new script. The introduction by Jeong In-ji talks about the excellence of the new script, King Sejong's great wisdom and other features. This section goes into greater detail about the "Haerye."

"Jejahae": Explanation of the principles behind the design of the letters

The first chapter in the "Jejahae" section gives a basic explanation of the new script and the principles behind its design. The academic background to Hangeul is Chinese phonology and Song Dynasty Neo-Confucianism, and explanations of the new script were given in this context. That is, since yin and yang and the five elements, as well as the great absolute, were principles used to explain all things in the universe, the sounds made by human beings and the writing they used were also explained with the same principles. As the principles behind sound were the same as those for writing, the new writing system was created according to the principles of sound.

Bilabial sounds

These are the sounds made when the mouth is closed then opened and are depicted using the letter ㅁ. To depict the shape of the lips parting when the mouth opens the letter ㅂ was created, while the letter ㅍ depicts the lips spreading sideways.

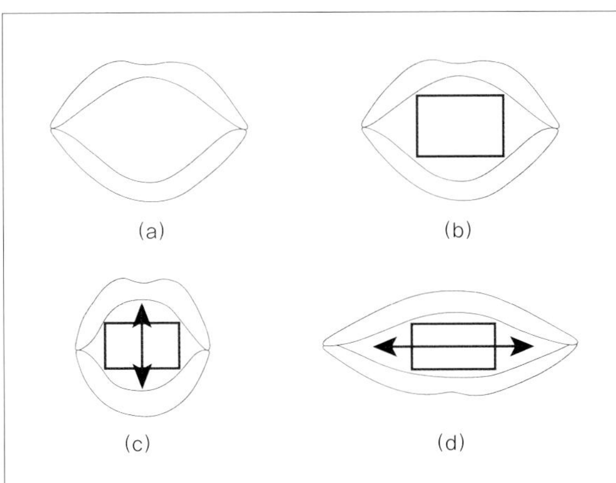

Alveolar sounds

These are the sounds made when the tongue touches the alveolar ridge (upper palate) and comes down again. The shape of the tongue in this action is depicted by the letter ㄴ. From this the letters ㄷ and ㅌ were made to reflect the shape of the speech organ and position of the tongue at the time of articulation.

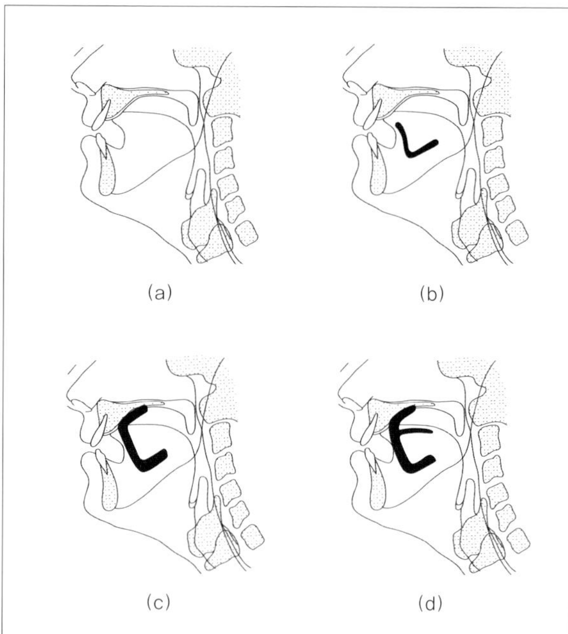

Velar sounds

These are the sounds made when the root of the tongue blocks the throat and is then released. The letters ㄱ and ㅋ were made to depict the shape of the tongue in this position.

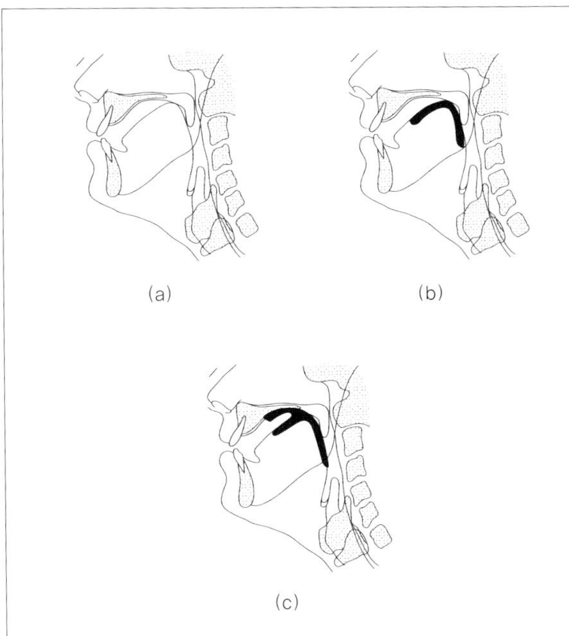

Dental sounds

These are the sounds made when the tongue moves between the upper and lower teeth or towards the back of the upper teeth. To reflect these sounds the letters ㅅ, ㅈ, ㅊ, and ㅿ were created. The triangle is no longer used today.

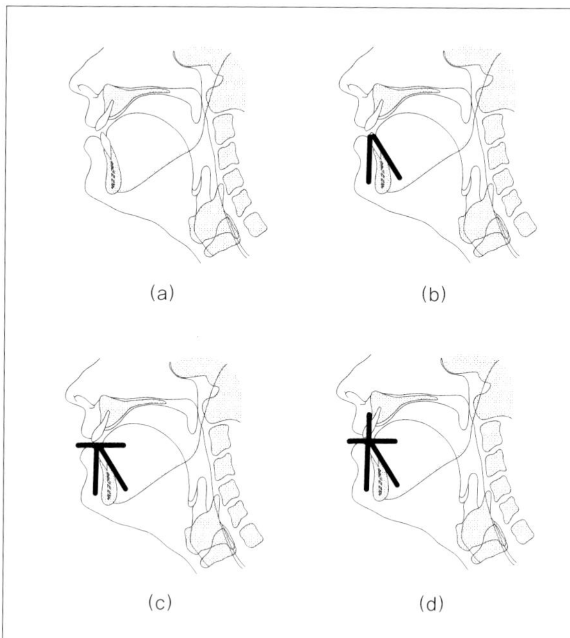

Glottal sounds

These are the sounds made from the throat. The letters ㅇ, ㆆ, and ㅎ were created to depict the outline of the throat and the shape of the speech organs.

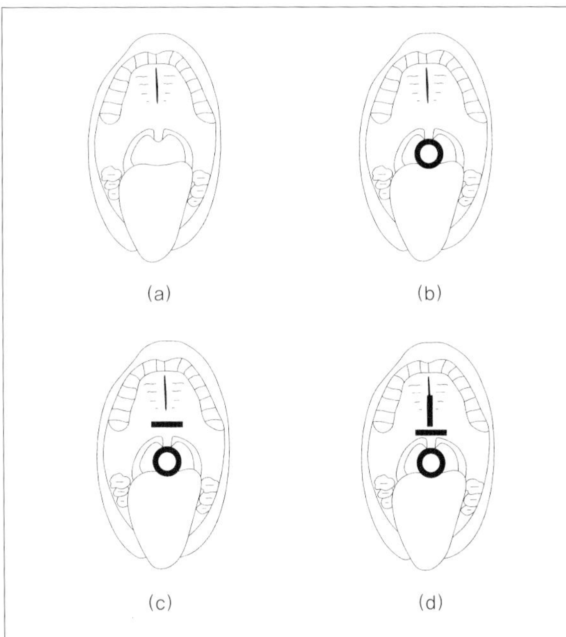

The consonants of similar shape were grouped together (including the fortis sounds), that is, those with the basic shape ㅇ, those with the basic shape ㅁ, those with the basic shape ㅅ, those with the basic shape ㄴ, and those with the basic shape ㄱ, in that order. If they are arranged in the order of simple to complex they are as follows:

ㅇ	ㅎ			
ㅁ	ㅂ	ㅍ	// ㅃ	
ㅅ	ㅈ	ㅊ	// ㅆ	ㅉ
ㄴ	ㄷ	ㅌ	// ㄸ	
ㄹ				
	ㄱ	ㅋ	// ㄲ	

Compound letters

The "Jejahae" section explains that a sound is made by joining the initial sound, medial sound and the final sound, and clarifies the function of each part. The sound begins with the initial sound and ends with the final sound while the medial sound is the center of the syllable. For example, ㄱ and ㅏ are combined to form 가, and if ㄱ and ㅏ and ㅁ are combined then they form the syllable 감. That is, the syllable starts with ㄱ and ends with ㅁ, while ㅏ is at the center.

Design of the final sounds

For the final sounds, the initial letters were repeated rather than creating a new set of separate letters. This is an accurate reflection of Korean words, where the initial sound of a syllable is often the same as the final one and vice versa. For example, in 밥도 the final ㅂ in 밥 is actually the final sound, but in 밥이, when the final ㅂ is joined with a postposition that starts with a vowel (이), the final ㅂ functions as the initial sound of the next syllable, which is transformed into a consonant: 바비. That is, the final sound sometimes functions as the initial sound, and initial sounds that have turned into consonants, depending on the circumstances, may also act as final sounds. Hence there was no need to create new letters for the final sounds.

"Choseonghae": Explanation of initial sounds

The *Hunmin jeongeum* explains that *choseong*, which means "initial sound," is equivalent in concept to the initial consonants (*zimu*) mentioned in Chinese rhyme books. It also explains its position in the syllable and gives concrete examples of the phonetic value of the 23 letters of the initial sound system of Hangeul. The explanation of velar sounds is as follows:

> The velar sound 군 is a compound of the basic consonant ㄱ as the initial sound combined with ᅮᆫ. In the case of 쾌, the initial sound ㅋ is combined with ᅫ. In the case of 뀨, the initial sound ㄲ is combined with ᅲ and in the case of 업, ㆁ is combined with ᅥᆸ.

"Jungseonghae": Explanation of medial sounds (vowels)

The "Jungseonghae" section explains the concept and function of medial sounds as the center of the syllable and how the syllable is created in combination with the initial and final consonants. It also explains the phonetic values of medial sounds using Chinese characters. It also shows how the three basic vowels generate four primary vowels and four secondary vowels to create eleven vowels, and how these can generate even further compound vowels as follows. (For the sake of convenience of printing, the compound vowels are depicted as they are used today.)

basic vowels	ㆍ	ㅡ	ㅣ			
primary vowels	ㅗ	ㅏ	ㅜ	ㅓ		
secondary vowels	ㅛ	ㅑ	ㅠ	ㅕ		
compound vowels	ㅘ	ㅝ	ㆇ	ㆊ		
vowels combined with ㅣ	ㆎ	ㅢ	ㅚ	ㅐ	ㅟ	ㅔ
	ㆉ	ㅒ	ㆌ	ㅖ		
	ㅙ	ㅞ	ㆈ	ㆋ		

The basic principle behind the formation of compound vowels is the combination of strokes of similar type. For example, medial vowels combined with the basic ㅣ vowel are described as being "pronounced by flattening the tongue and because the sound is shallow it is easy to open the mouth."

"Jongseonghae": Explanation of final sounds (consonants)

The "Jongseonghae" section explains the position and function of the *jongseong*, or final consonant: the final consonant comes after the initial and medial sounds and completes the rhyme. The important thing here is the division of the syllable into three parts. The Chinese people divided each sound into two parts, the *seong* (tone) and *un* (rhyme) but the "Haerye" shows that Koreans divided each syllable into three parts – initial, medial and final sounds – which were treated together as one whole.

Next, the "Jongseonghae" explains the types of final consonants as entering tones[18] or non-entering tones[19] according to the sound of the consonant at the end of the syllable. For example, as ㄱ is a closed

18. One of the four tones of Chinese characters, it is short sound that ends quickly.
19. Non-entering tones, that is, level, rising and departing tones

Scholars of Jiphyeonjeon. King Sejong Memorial Society

sound, it can only be an entering tone, and as ㅇ has the nasal cavity wide open, it cannot be an entering tone.

However, "Jongseonghae" explained that there were only eight consonants that were true final consonants. It also explains that consonants such as ㅅ, ㅈ, △, ㅊ, etc. could all be represented as ㅅ in the final position, according to the principle of the eight final consonants, which are ㄱ, ㄴ, ㄷ, ㄹ, ㅁ, ㅂ, ㅅ and ㆁ.

In the Korean language, even without the addition of ㅇ in the final position, "Jongseonghae" states the syllable could be produced by the medial vowel without the final sound. This suggests that the Joseon scholars of that time, under the influence of Chinese phonology (*sheng yunxue*), perceived the need for final consonants. This perception is also reflected in the fact that the ㅇ was later added to the group of final consonants.

Aside from ㄱ and ㆁ, which were first introduced in the "Jongseonghae," examples of the remaining consonants, that is, ㄷ, ㄴ, ㅂ, ㅁ, ㅅ, and ㄹ, are given.

"Hapjahae": Explanation of the combination of letters

This section explains how the letters of Hangeul are used in combination with each other.

Composition of the syllables

The initial, medial and final sounds are joined together to create one syllable. In regard to the compound of initial and medial sounds, "Hapjahae" explains which vowels are used next to the initial sound and which letters are used underneath.

Medials used next to initial sounds · ㅡ ㅗ ㅛ ㅜ ㅠ

Medials used underneath initial sounds ㅣ ㅏ ㅑ ㅓ ㅕ

Stipulating that the final sound is used below the initial and medial sound, it shows by way of example that when ㄴ is placed underneath 구 (*gu*), it becomes 군 (*gun*).

Initial compounds

This section shows how two letters or three letters can be used in combination in the initial position.

Lateral placement of different characters ㅅㄷ ㅂㅈ ㅂㅅㄱ
Lateral placement of same characters ㆅ ㆀ ㅆ

Examples of the former include those starting with ㅅ or ㅂ, or ㅄ. The three examples of the latter are those that were commonly used in the Korean language.

Medial compounds

This section gives examples of two or three letters used together in the medial position.

Two-letter compound ㅘ(과)
Three-letter compound ㆇ(홰)

Final compounds

This section gives examples of two or three letters used together in the final position.

Two-letter compound ㄺ ㄱㅅ
Three-letter compound ㄹㄱㅅ

It is supposed that these are examples of real sounds at the time. That is, it is presumed three-letter compounds such as ᇌ were really articulated at the time.

Miscellaneous compounds

This refers to compounds consisting of Chinese characters and Hangeul mixed together. In such cases, according to the sound of the Chinese character used, the compound can be articulated in medial position or in final position.

Medial articulation	孔子ㅣ
Final articulation	魯ㅅ(사ᄅᆞᆷ)

While the sound of the Chinese character 子 finishes in a vowel sound, in combination with ㅣ, it becomes a double vowel with a descending tone and ㅣ is articulated in medial position. When a character ending with a vowel sound is used in combination with a consonant, the consonant is articulated in final position.

Addition of dots

This section explains how variations in tone were expressed with the addition of dots.

1 dot	departing tone
2 dots	rising tone
no dots	level tone

Common Usage

This section explains that in initial position, ㆆ is considered the same as ㅇ.

Yeonseo (letters placed on top of each other)

In the case of semi-lingual sounds there are so-called "light sounds" and "heavy sounds." It was explained that if they were to be spoken they could be used by placing ㅇ underneath, as in the case of the light labial sound.

Light labial sound ㅸ
Light liquid sound ᄛ

Dialect and children's language

There were two vowel sounds that existed at the time to express regional dialects or the language of children, although they were not included in the common list of compound vowels. They are letters which contain ㅣ and · together on top of each other and those that contain ㅣ and ㅡ on top of each other.

"Yongjarye": Examples of the letters in use

This part gives an explanation of native Korean words using single letters. For example, with the initial consonants, aside from the character ㆆ and including the *yeonseo* sound ㅸ, it presents two examples each for the 17 letters invented. In the case of the medial vowels, there are four examples for each of the eleven vowels created. And for the eight final consonants that are actually articulated, as described in "Jongseonghae," it gives two examples for each.

Ⅲ. Dissemination and Spread of Hangeul

Hangeul, a new script for the Korean language, was created in 1444 during the reign of King Sejong under the name "Hunmin jeongeum." It faced opposition from the conservatives and the court in general, but it continued to grow in influence. Although Choe Man-ri and other conservatives raised strong objections to the script in the early days, all kinds of books were published in Hangeul, including translations of Chinese books. Moreover, part of the *Hunmin jeongeum* manuscript was included as a subject in the state civil service exams, enhancing its authority, and various textbooks for the study of Chinese characters and Chinese as well as other foreign languages were written in Hangeul, which naturally widened its influence.

During the reign of Yeonsangun, the suppression of Hangeul temporarily posed an obstacle to its spread. But when the Four Books and Three Classics (compulsory texts for the state civil service exams) were translated and transcribed in Hangeul, those sitting for the exams could not avoid reading these Confucian texts in Hangeul. With the spread of Hangeul to the ordinary people, the new script became a part of everyday life.

1. Dissemination of Hangeul
2. Hangeul-related Cultural Heritage
3. Spread of Hangeul in Everyday Life

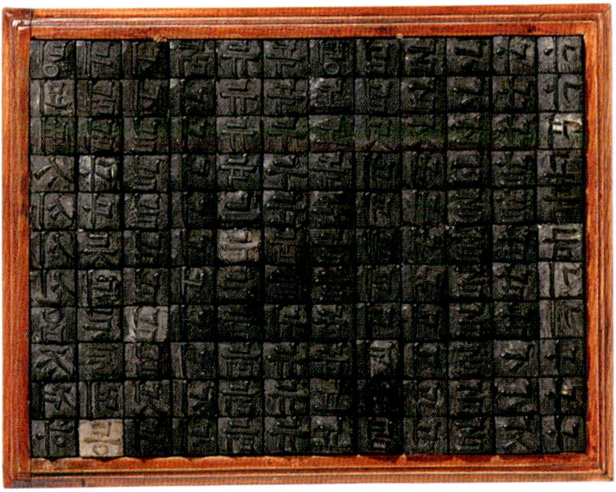

Hangeul metal type. National Museum of Korea

1. Dissemination of Hangeul

When Hangeul was created in 1444 under the name Hunmin jeongeum, it was also called by a variety of other names such as "Jeongeum," "Eonmun" and "Banjeol." The name Eonmun is mentioned in the *Annals of King Sejong (Sejong sillok)*, and is understood to mean "a script for expression of the language of everyday life."

In 1445, King Sejong compiled the epic poem *Songs of the Flying Dragons (Yongbi eocheonga)*. Comprising 125 pages, it was published in 1447 as the first piece of literature to combine Chinese characters with Hangeul. King Sejong then commissioned a translation of *Illustrated Guide to the Three Bonds (Samgang haengsildo)* from Chinese to Hangeul so that "all uneducated people young and old, male and female can easily understand its meaning" (*Annals of King Sejong*, 26th year of Sejong). Many other books including rhyme books, Buddhist sutras and literary works were translated into Hangeul during the succeeding reigns of kings Munjong, Danjong, Sejo, and Seongjong.

To promote practical use of Hangeul, it was occasionally included as a subject in the state civil service exams. Although King Yeonsangun closed down Eonmuncheong (Office of the Hunmin jeongeum) in 1504 and banned the use or teaching of Hangeul, publication of a book in Hangeul explaining the *Thousand Character Classic* meant that use of the Korean script inevitably spread among the ruling and upper classes.

When *gasa*, a type of free-form poetry, began to thrive after the mid-Joseon period, literary works written in Hangeul grew popular, a few notable examples being the novels *The Story of Hong Gil-dong (Honggildong-jeon), The Story of Simcheong (Simcheong-jeon)* and *The Story of Chunhyang (Chunhyang-jeon)*. Moreover, when the king's words began to be officially recorded or explained in Hangeul, the new script became more firmly established and started to emerge as part of the common people's everyday lives.

Works written in Hangeul

Yongbi eocheonga: Song in praise of kings

Yongbi eocheonga (*Songs of the Flying Dragons*) is the first poem written with the use of Hangeul. In 1445, following the creation of Hunmin jeongeum, a group of prominent scholars including Gwon Je, Jeong In-ji, An Ji, Park Paeng-nyeon, Kang Hui-an, Sin Suk-ju, Yi Hyeon-ro, Seong Sam-mun, Yi Gae, and Sin Yeong-son wrote a 125-page poetic song and presented it to the king. King Sejong was highly pleased with the work and named it *Yongbi eocheonga*. It is an epic poem that sings the praises of six generations of Sejong's royal ancestors, from Mokjo of Goryeo (great-great-grandfather of Yi Seong-gye, founder of Joseon) to Sejong's father King Taejong. These direct ancestors of Sejong were deemed to have acted under the command of heaven, which was a way of emphasizing that they were on a par with the emperors of China. Written one year before Hunmin Jeongeum was officially promulgated, *Yongbi eocheonga* was the first published work to use the new script.

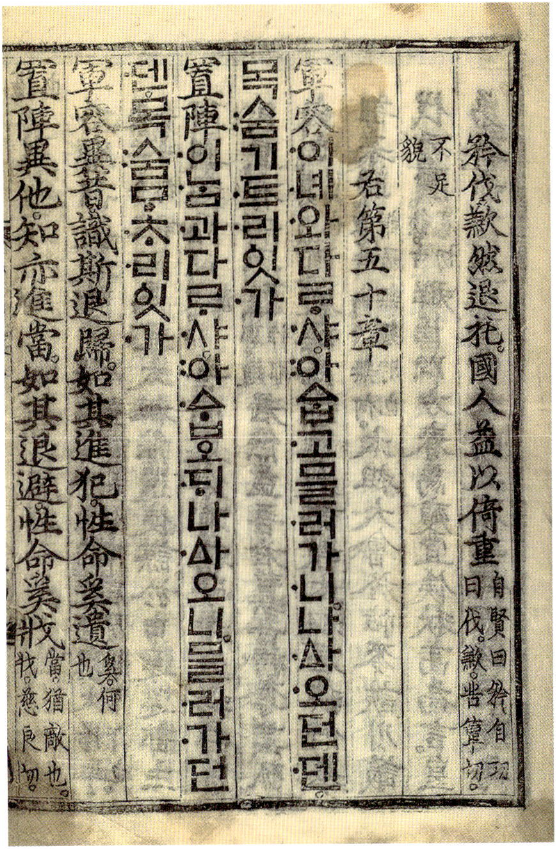

Yongbi eocheonga (Songs of the Flying Dragons). 1447. Woodblock print. Bumwoosa Publishing Co.

Dongguk jeongun (Standard Rhymes of the Eastern State). National Treasure No.142. Konkuk University Museum

Dongguk jeongun: Organization of sounds

In 1448, two years after the proclamation of Hunmin jeongeum, King Sejong commissioned Sin Suk-ju, Choe Hang, Park Paeng-nyeon and other scholars to write *Dongguk jeongun (Standard Rhymes of the Eastern State)*, Korea's first rhyme dictionary. Two extant copies of the six-volume book have been respectively designated National Treasure No. 71 (Vol. 1, 6 preserved at Kansong Art Museum) and National Treasure No. 142 (preserved at Konkuk University Museum).

The year after the Hunmin jeongeum was completed, King Sejong, in consultation with the Office of Deliberation (Uisacheong), had the rhyme dictionary *Yunhui* translated into Hangeul, despite the opposition of Choe Man-ri and others. Some of the most important rhyme dictionaries published during the reign of King Sejong were *Saseong tonggo, Hongmujeongun yeokhun*, and *Dongguk jeongun.*

Seokbo sangjeol: Stories about the Buddha

Seokbo sangjeol, or *Episodes from the Life of Buddha*, published in 1447, is a book containing stories about Sakyamuni and edited versions of the Buddhist sutras, compiled by Prince Suyang, Kim Su-on and others. The project was established to pray for Queen Soheon's peace in the afterlife and to convert the people to Buddhism.

The state civil service exams and spread of Hangeul

Gwageo

Gwageo is the name of the exams held to select men to serve as government officials. This exam system originated in China, and came to Korea in 788, 4th year of the reign of King Wonseong of Silla, who held national exams called *dokseo sampumgwa*. In the Goryeo Dynasty, King Gwangjong held *gwageo* exams in 958.

In the Joseon Dynasty, the exam was held in two divisions: the literary exams (*mungwa*) and the military exams (*mugwa*). The literary exams were held in two levels: the lower exams being called *sogwa* to select lower-level officials, and the higher exams *daegwa* for high-level officials. The *sogwa* were further divided into the classics licentiate exam (*saengwongwa*), the literary licentiate exam (*jinsagwa*), and the *japgwa* for technical officials such as translators, doctors, scientists and legal officials.

Hunmin jeongeum as an exam subject

In 1446, not long after the promulgation of Hangeul, the king instructed that "From now on, when selecting scribes and lower officials, their knowledge of the *Hunmin jeongeum* should also be tested. Although a person may not know the meanings and principles if he can use the letters, recruit him."

In the fourth month of the following year, he instructed that Hangeul tests be strengthened in a broad range of exams. This can be confirmed in the following record from the sixth year of the reign of the King Sejo.

> "... the *Hunmin jeongeum* was created by the earlier King Sejong, *Dongguk jeongun* and *Hongmu jeongun* were compiled by the king, and *Imun* is essential for the ruling class. From now on, in the first exam for civil officials we will test them in debate of these three books, and rank them according to their results in the Four Books and Five Classics. In the final examination we will add *Imun* as an exam subject and rank them according to the solutions they suggest to political or administrative problems."

Use of Hangeul in the court

As explained above, the new script became an exam subject in the civil service exams, and was a tool for translation of Chinese-character texts into Korean. These circumstances had the effect of expanding the use of Hangeul. Hence from the beginning, the use of Hangeul grew in scope. Concrete examples of the use of Hangeul in the court follow, including instructions from the king regarding affairs of state and matters that had to be communicated to the king, and communication among people of the court.

The king's work and related affairs

King Sejong had his official commands written in Hangeul.

> "The king listened to the crimes of all the officials of the Office of the Inspector General [Saheonbu] and the Office of Censors [Saganwon]

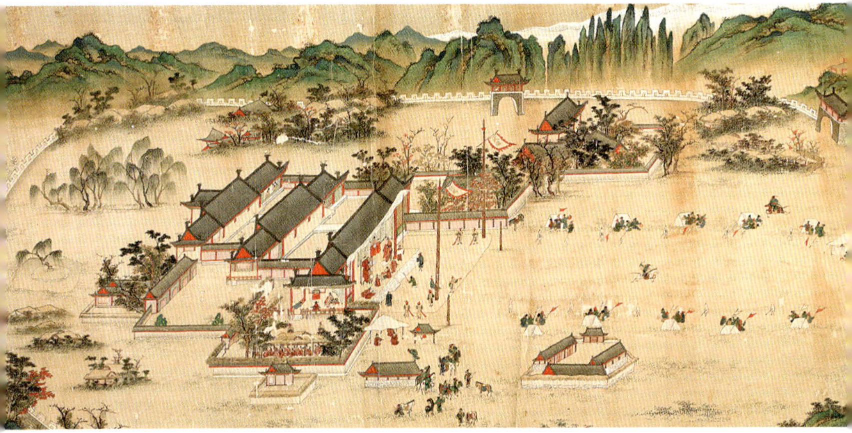

State Civil Service Exams in Hamheung. National Museum of Korea

and wrote them down in Eonmun [Hangeul] and commanded that the court attendant Kim Deuk-sang show them to the Royal Bureau of Investigation [Uigeumbu] and the Royal Secretariat [Seungjeongwon]." (*Annals of King Sejong*, 1446)

Also, letters from officials to the king were written in Hangeul. The following record remains regarding a letter sent by Prince Yang-nyeong to King Munjong.

Prince Yangnyeong Yi Je wrote a short letter written in Eonmun requesting that [his brother-in-law] Kim Gyeong-jae be permitted to return to Seoul and be present at the marriage of his daughter. The matter has been turned over to the cabinet for discussion. (*Annals of King Munjong*, 1451)

Hangeul for communication in the palace

Hangeul was also used as a means of communication inside the royal palace, as seen in letters from female court attendants to Lady Hyebin (mother of King Jeongjo), and in letters between court attendants themselves. The following attests to the use of Hangeul in a letter to Lady Hyebin.

> Among the court attendants, some stayed at Sugang Palace and one of them wrote a letter in Eonmun to Lady Hyebin asking after the welfare of her wet nurse, and Lady Hyebin passed the letter on to Naejeon [inner court, for the women of the palace]. From Naejeon the letter was sent to the Royal Secretariat [Seungjeongwon] and the contents are as follows: "Myodan said that Jageum, Jungbi and Gaji, who are all female attendants in the court, are seeking to commit adultery with *byeolgam* [low officials]." So Yi Ye-jang from the State Council [Uijeongbu] was summoned to discuss the problem with *dangsang* [high officials].

Limitations in dissemination of Hangeul

Perception of the scholars

The creation of a new script was controversial from the start. At a time when Joseon looked up to greater powers (China), the creation of a new script that would decisively affect literacy based on the use of Chinese characters meant the overturning of existing values. In addition, the absence of texts written in the new script created barriers to learning. The objections of Choe Man-ri, who headed Jiphyeonjeon at the time, and scholars who supported him, are well captured in the so-called "Choe Man-ri appeal" as follows:

> I do not place importance in whether achievements are made quickly or slowly, but these days the nation is striving to deal with all things with speed. This worries me as it seems to go against the spirit of politics. If there is no choice but to create Eonmun, its impact is significant as it means changing all customs and must be discussed with all officials from the prime minister down. Even if all the people say it is right, we should think carefully before acting and then think about it again three more times.

The above reflects a conservative attitude and a warning not to change tradition too hastily. The following passage expresses the view that the creation of Eonmun is neither urgent nor helpful in learning or study.

> Past scholars have said that "Love of many varied pursuits leads to a lack of resolve" and that "While the writing of letters is one of the major pursuits of the scholar, a penchant for such pursuit alone also weakens resolve." Though the crown prince has attained much virtue, he must concentrate on the teaching of the sages and study harder to achieve the things not yet attained. While Eonmun may be useful, [writing] is only one of the six arts of the man of letters. Moreover, if by chance it is of no benefit in politics, and time is wasted on learning it and thinking about it, it would certainly be a loss at a time when study is important.

Such perceptions of the new script proved to be obstacles in spreading Eonmun and establishing its use among the upper class of Joseon.

Violent rule of Yeonsangun and suppression of Hangeul

Some sixty years after the creation of Hangeul, an incident arose that decisively deterred the spread of the new script. With the death of King Seongjong in the 12th month of 1494, Prince Yeonsangun rose to the throne and reigned for twelve years until he was ousted in the Jungjong Restoration in 1506. The beginning of Yeonsangun's reign was peaceful with the officials from Seongjong's time remaining active. But in the fourth year, Yeonsangun's corrupt nature began to show and he eventually brought great misery upon the nation. The first literati purge took place in 1498 and the second literati purge in 1504, and while they were both related to factional strife at the time, they were largely brought about by Yeonsangun's weaknesses as a ruler and his own tyrannical character. In the first purge, the body of the renowned early Joseon Neo-Confucian scholar Kim Jong-jik was dug up from his grave and defiled, and his disciples were executed. In the second purge, two concubines of Yeonsangun's father, King Seongjong, were dragged out into the palace grounds and beaten to death, and his grandmother was also killed in a similar fashion. His deeds left great wounds on the nation, both morally and politically.

Under such circumstances, there was ceaseless conflict between the king and the officials. The advisory officials who believed it their bounden duty to speak the truth, continued to remonstrate the king. But Yeonsangun, finding this tiresome, simply got rid of the two advisory offices Saganwon and Hongmungwan. He also abolished all institutions and systems that allowed people to express their opinions, such as written appeals by officials to the king and the beating of a drum by members of the public to stop the king's procession and appeal to him directly. Moreover, he also used Seonggyungwan, the national Confucian academy, as a place where he drank and was attended by women, and turned Wongaksa Temple, which had flourished as the center of the Jogye Order of Buddhism, into a *gisaeng* house (pleasure venue) named Yeonbangwon.

Yeonsangun did not stop there. He turned Heungcheonsa Temple, headquarters of the *seon* sect of Buddhism, into stables, and changed the Office of the Humin jeongeum into an office in charge of *gisaeng* (professional female entertainers) related matters. When an anonymous notice written in Hangeul criticizing the king was posted, Yeonsangun banned the use of Hangeul and went to all lengths to find the offender.

The ruinous situation was finally upturned in the ninth month of 1506 when Seong Hui-an, Park Won-jong, Yu Sun-jeong and others, deposed Yeonsangun, and his younger brother, Prince Jinseong (later King Jungjong), was placed on the throne instead.

Revival of Hangeul

Even after the creation of Hangeul, the state civil service exams and education at Seonggyungwan continued to be based on literary Chinese. The ruling class concentrated on learning Chinese characters and had little interest in Hangeul. Of course, Hangeul was around only 50 years old during Yeonsangun's reign and there had been little time for dissemination of the new script. The situation can be surmised from the fact that Yeonsangun ordered a list to be drawn up of all the people who were familiar with Hangeul and had their handwriting compared with that on the anonymous notice criticizing him. Such a project was possible because the number of people who knew Hangeul was not that large.

A breakthrough in the spread of Hangeul came when Hangeul started to be used in textbooks for the study of Chinese characters and foreign languages. The appearance of books containing explana-

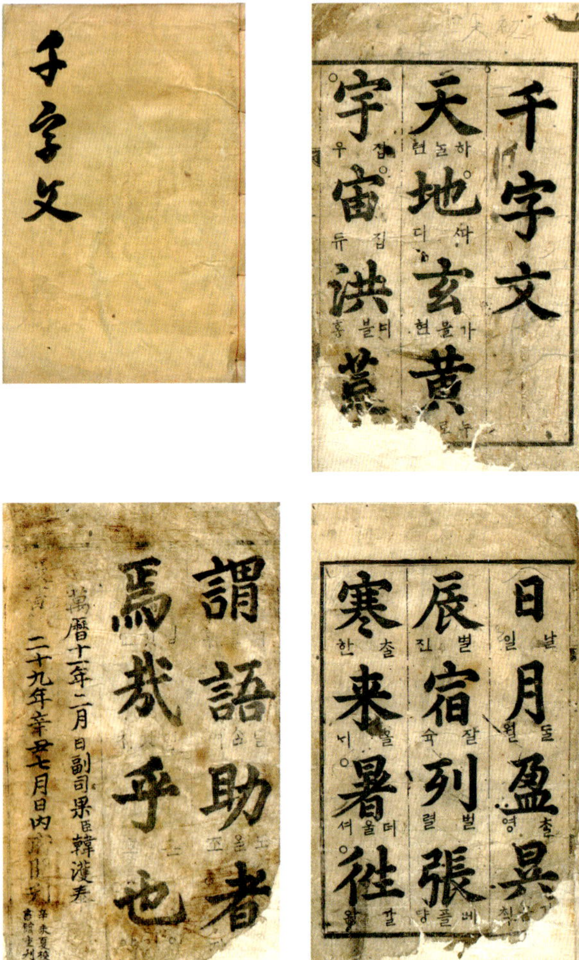

Thousand Character Classic, Korea University Library

tions of the meanings and sounds of Chinese characters written in Hangeul and foreign language textbooks with content transcribed in Hangeul forced those studying literary Chinese or foreign languages to learn the new script.

Chinese-character education and the spread of Hangeul

According to the preface of Choe Se-jin's *Collection of Characters for Training the Unenlightened (Hunmong jahoe)* from the early Joseon period, study of Chinese characters began with the *Thousand Character Classic* followed by *Yuhap*. The *Thousand Character Classic* is a Chinese book that was brought into Korea while *Yuhap* is a text published in Korea explaining the meanings and sounds of Chinese characters. The authorship of *Yuhap* is disputed. Some say it was written by Seo Geo-jeong during the reign of King Seongjong of Joseon while others refute this argument. Whatever the case, these two textbooks served not only to teach Chinese characters but to also spread Hangeul among the ruling class.

The most prominent version of the *Thousand Character Classic*, called *Cheonjamun* in Korean, was that written by the famed calligrapher Han Ho (1543–1605). This book, containing Han Ho's handwriting, was first published in 1583 and reissued several times afterwards. *Cheonjamun* was structured so that the pronunciation of the Chinese character for "heaven" (天) was explained in Hangeul. Hence everyone who studied the book had to first learn Hangeul. *Yuhap* was a book studied by those who had finished *Cheonjamun* and likewise contained explanations of meanings and sounds that were written in Hangeul.

Choe Se-jin was one of Joseon's foremost scholars in Chinese-character phonology. He died in 1542 but his date of birth is unknown. During his lifetime Choe wrote seven books and translated another ten books. In addition to *Collection of Characters for Training the Unenlightened*, some of his major works that remain important to this day are *Thorough Investigation of the Four Tones (Saseong tonghae)*, *Korean Translation of Nogeoldae (Beonyeok nogeoldae)*, *Korean Translation of Baktongsa (Beonyeok baktongsa)*, and *Imun jimnam*. These are books from the early and mid-16th century on the Korean language, Chinese linguistics and Chinese character phonology.

Korean Translation of Nogeoldae and *Korean Translation of Baktongsa* are Chinese language textbooks that required readers to first learn Hangeul in order to study Chinese. *Imun jimnam* is a text that interprets difficulties in the language used for official documents (Imun) and also required an understanding of Hangeul.

The textbook *Collection of Characters for Training the Unenlightened* was written in Hangeul by Choe Se-jin in 1527 and carries explanations of the meanings and sounds of 3,360 Chinese characters. The necessity of learning Hangeul (Eonmun) to study Chinese characters is mentioned in the book.

> As there are many people in rural areas and the provinces who do not know Eonmun, if the Eonmun letters are also written down in the book so that Eonmun may be learnt before studying *Collection of Characters for Training the Unenlightened*, it may be helpful in bringing enlightenment. Those who do not know Chinese characters, if they learn Eonmun first and then study Chinese characters, even without a teacher they will be able to understand Chinese characters.

Foreign language education and Hangeul

As many foreign language textbooks came to be written in Hangeul, anyone wanting to learn a foreign language inevitably had to first learn Hangeul. Chinese language study books include *Korean*

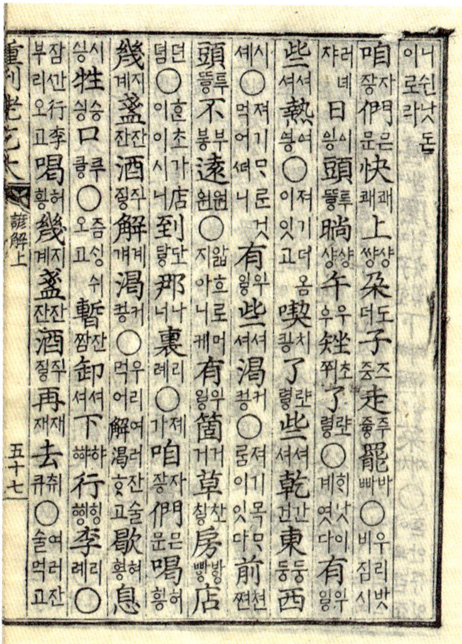

***Nogeoldae eonhae* *(Annotated Nogeoldae)*.**
1795. Woodblock print.
Bumwoosa Publishing Co.

Translation of Nogeoldae, *Korean Translation of Baktongsa*, as discussed above, as well as *Korean Translation of Two Brothers and the Five Confucian Virtues (Oryun jeonbi eonhae)*. Japanese language textbooks include *Cheophae sineo* and *Iropa*. There was also a Mongolian language textbook, *Mongeo nogeoldae*, and the Manchurian language textbook *Cheongeo nogeoldae*.

Korean annotation of the Seven Books and spread of Hangeul

The Seven Books refer to the Four Books and Three Classics of Confucianism. The Four Books are the *Great Learning*, *Doctrine of the*

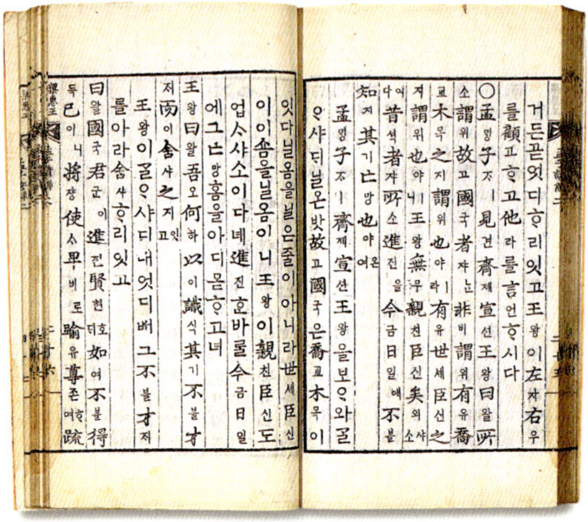

Maengja eonhae (Korean Translation of the Mencius), National Museum of Korea

Korean Translation of the Poems of Du Fu, 1632, National Museum of Korea

Mean, Analects of Confucius, the *Mencius*, while the Three Classics are the *Classic of Poetry (Shijing)*, the *Classic of History (Shujing)*, and the *Book of Changes (I Ching)*. In Korea, the compilation of these seven books with Hangeul annotation is called *Chilseo eonhae*.

Translation of the Seven Books into Hangeul began in the King Sejong era but remained unfinished for a long time. The project was finally completed in 1588 during the reign of King Seonjo. Because the Seven Books were mandatory texts for the state civil service exams, their translation meant that all members of the ruling class who sat for the exams to become government officials learnt Hangeul. While all texts in literary Chinese, including the Confucian classics, lend themselves to varied interpretation, translations commissioned by the court provided a standard interpretation.

Active use of Hangeul in the court

The king, the highest authority in the land, often exchanged correspondence with his children in Hangeul. The queen also did the same. That the royal family, symbol of authority in the Joseon Dynasty, wrote letters in Hangeul was meant to serve as a model for all the people, and suggested that ordinary individuals were also in the habit of using Hangeul for personal correspondence.

The photo on the following page is a letter written by King Seonjo in 1603 to his daughter Princess Jeongsuk. It clearly reflects the father's concern for his sick daughter. The next photo is a letter exchanged by King Hyojong and his daughter Princess Sungmyeong, asking about each other's welfare.

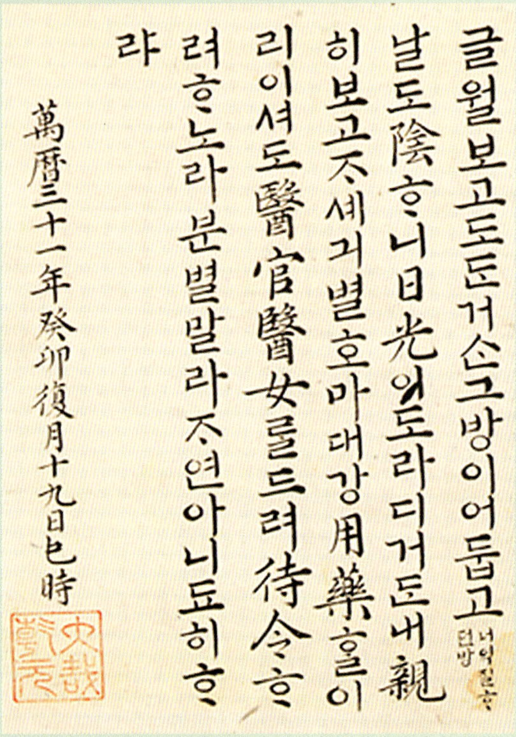

Letter from King Seonjo to his daughter Princess Jeongsuk, 1603, Kyujanggak Institute for Korean Studies

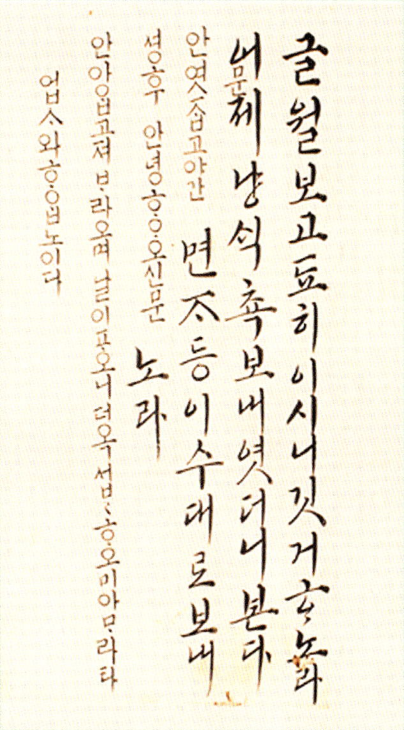

글월보고 됴히 이시니 깃거ᄒᆞ노라
어제 냥식 쵹보내엿더니 본다
안엿ᄌᆞᆸ고야간 면ᄌᆞ등이 수대로 보내
셩후 안녕ᄒᆞ오신문 노라
안아옵고져 ᄇᆞ라오며 날이 ᄎᆞ오니 더옥 섭섭ᄒᆞ오미 아므라타
업ᄉᆞ와ᄒᆞ옵노이다

Correspondence between King Hyojong and his daughter Princess Sungmyeong, National Museum of Korea

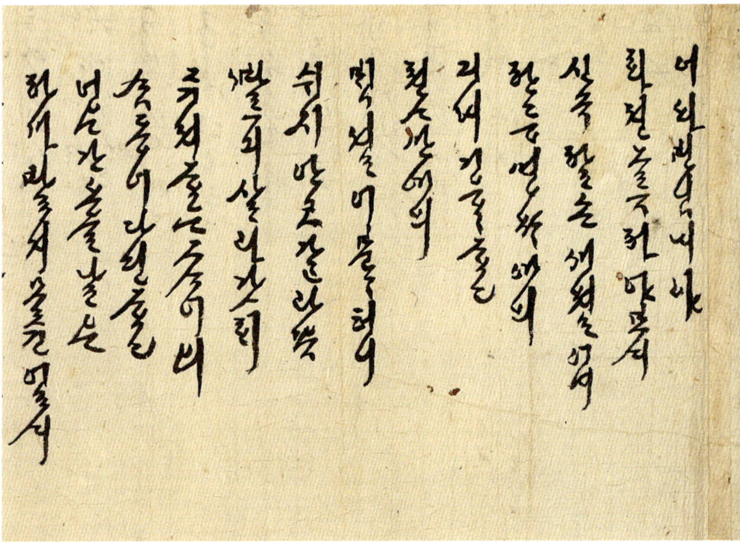

Hwajeon-ga (Song of the Flower Cakes), 1814, National Museum of Korea

2. Hangeul-related Cultural Heritage

Publication of *sijo* collections

Sijo is a form of native Korean poetry that emerged in the late Goryeo period. *Sijo* established a standardized format, and it can be said that all preceding Korean poetry was a precursor to the *sijo* form and that all poetry afterwards originated from it. As the major form of native Korean literature, *sijo* has expressed the spirit and sentiment of the Korean people for almost one thousand years. From the mid-Joseon period, collections of *sijo* translated into Hangeul were compiled, which enabled them to be shared among the common people and passed down to this day, conveying the sentiments of the Korean people across the ages.

Cheonggu yeongeon: *Enduring Poetry of Korea*

This is a collection of *sijo* from the late Goryeo period to the time of its compilation in 1728 by the poet Kim Cheon-taek. This anthology is the oldest and largest collection of *sijo* handed down to the present. The first edition was published in 1727 (3rd year of King Yeongjo), the first supplemented edition in 1728, and the second supplemented edition in 1732. It appears a significant number of poems were added in the first supplemented edition, so the anthology is considered to have been properly completed in 1728. There are seven different versions of the anthology: 1) Choe Nam-seon version, 2) Oh Jang-hwan version, 3) Lee Hui-seung version, 4) Hong Jae-hyu version, 5) Lee Byeong-gi version, 6) Yi Ga-won version, and 7) Ogura Shinpei and Fujita (Japanese authors) version. As an example of the breadth of the collection, the Choe Nam-seon version contains 999 *sijo* as well as 16 *gasa* (another form of poetic song popular in the Joseon period).

Haedong gayo: Songs of Korea

This is one of the three major poetry anthologies of the Joseon period, compiled by the singer and poet Kim Su-jang. Started in 1746, the first phase of the collection was completed in 1755. The second phase was completed in 1763 and given the name *Haedong gayo*. It was continually supplemented and edited through 1769, when Kim Su-jang turned 80. Two versions have been handed down to the present: the Yukdang version, which originally belonged to Choe Nam-seon and was later transcribed by the noted linguist Ju Si-gyeong; and the Gosa version, originally owned by Lee Hui-seung. The Yukdang version contains 568 *sijo*.

Gagok wollyu: Anthology of Korean Songs

This collection of *sijo* compiled by Park Hyo-gwan and An Min-yeong in 1876 contains some 800 poems, though there are differences according to the version. The writers span a time period of one thousand years, starting with Eulpaso (?–203) from the Goguryeo Kingdom to An Min-yeong from the Joseon Dynasty. The writers also cover a wide social spectrum with kings, noted officials and scholars at the top, and *gisaeng* (professional female entertainers) at the bottom. If the two abovementioned works *Cheonggu yeongeon* and

Haedong gayo can be likened to mid-term reports on *sijo*, *Gagok wollyu* can be seen as the overall final report on this literary genre.

Emergence of novels written in Hangeul

Honggildong-jeon: *The Story of Hong Gil-dong*

The first novel to be written in Hangeul is *The Story of Hong Gil-dong (Honggildong-jeon)* by the mid-Joseon writer Heo Gyun (1569–1618). Influenced by the Chinese novel *The Water Margin (Shui hu zhuan)*, the novel satirizes the paradoxes of Joseon's social systems following the Japanese invasions (1592–1598). The content can be summarized as follows:

> Hong Gil-dong, born of the concubine of Hong Mun, second state councilor during the reign of King Sejong of the Joseon Dynasty, is skilled in martial arts and Taoist magic arts but as the son of a concubine he is not permitted to take the state exams to become a military official. Gil-dong, lamenting his status as an illegitimate child unable to live with proper human dignity, leaves home after surviving an assassin attack plotted by another concubine of his father who is jealous of his talent. He runs into a band of thieves but ends up taking control and becoming their leader. Named Hwalbindang, the band of thieves focuses on robbing from corrupt government officials and monks. When their fame spreads across the country, the court sets out to catch Hong Gil-dong but fails. In an effort to conciliate, the king offers him a government position but Hong Gil-dong informs the king that he will leave the country with the members of Hwalbindang. Taking his mother, he then heads for a fictional land named Yuldo and establishes his own state.

Simcheong-jeon: The Story of Simcheong

Date and author unknown, this is the quintessential Korean classical novel. The underlying themes are the Confucian concept of filial piety and the Buddhist idea of reaping what you sow. Though dozens of different versions exist, there are two major types, those published in Seoul (Gyeongpan version) and those published in Jeonju (Wanpan version). The wide dissemination of Hangeul is evidenced by the numerous versions of this novel, which were read by all walks of society. The story is as follows:

> The dutiful daughter Simcheong sells herself to some fishermen as a sacrifice in exchange for 300 sacks of rice, which is offered to the Buddha to make her blind father see again. On the rough seas, Simcheong throws herself into the sea to appease the waters. But Simcheong is saved by the Dragon King of the Four Seas and becomes his queen. In order to find her father, Simcheong holds a banquet for all the blind people in the country. She is reunited with her father and her father is able to see again.

Chunhyang-jeon: The Story of Chunhyang

This story is the novel form of one of the twelve *pansori* (a form of musical story-telling) pieces known to have existed. Though surmised to date to the Yeongjo-Jeongjo era, its exact date of creation and author are unknown. The ideas of self-realization and making one's dreams come true that are reflected in the story struck a chord with the common people of the late Joseon period, while the heroine's romantic encounter with the hero and her fidelity and chastity fell in line with the moral principles of the time. *The Story of Chunhyang* was read by both the upper and lower classes alike. Indeed, it was a novel widely loved by all. There are some 70–

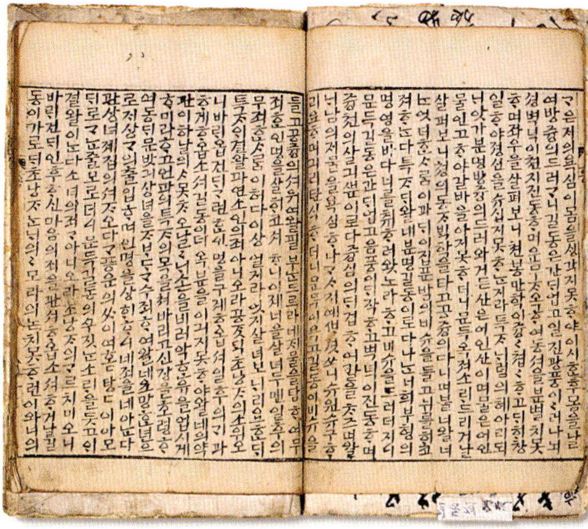

The Story of Hong Gil-dong, National Museum of Korea

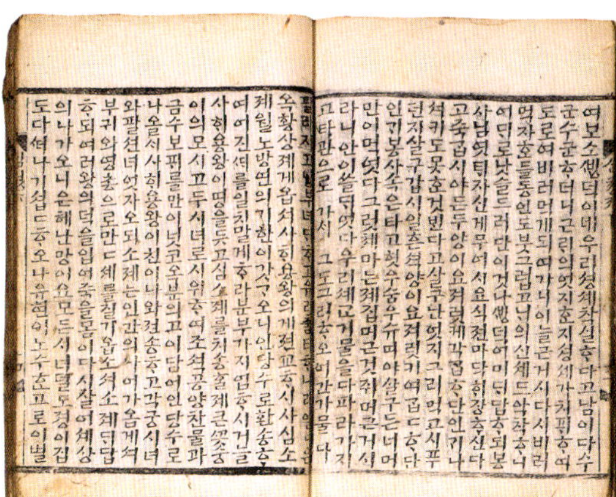

The Story of Simcheong, National Museum of Korea

Part of a folding screen depicting the meeting of Yi Mong-ryong and Chunhyang in *The Story of Chunhyang*, Central Museum of Kyunghee University

80 versions of this novel, including translations into foreign languages, which attests to the acceptance and spread of Hangeul.

In the early part of the reign of King Sukjong, a retired *gisaeng* named Wolmae living in Namwon and a high official by the name of Seong have a daughter named Chunhyang. Chunhyang is not only beautiful she is also highly accomplished at poetry and calligraphy. One beautiful spring day, Chunhyang is playing on the swing when she is spotted by Yi Mong-ryong, son of the Namwon magistrate. He falls in love at first sight and the two are betrothed to each other, with the permission of Wolmae. The young couple spend happy days together, but when his father is called back to the capital Yi Mong-ryong hurriedly departs, promising to return to fetch Chunhyang. The new magistrate, Byeon Hak-do, tries to force Chunhyang into his bed and when she refuses he orders her to be beaten and imprisoned. In Seoul, Yi Mong-ryong wins first place in the state civil service exams and returns to Namwon in disguise as the secret royal inspector. Before he reaches the city he hears of Chunhyang's plight and visits her in prison, but Chunhyang fails to recognize him. On his birthday, Byeon Hak-do holds a banquet and Yi Mong-ryong attends the party disguised as a beggar. There he writes a poem condemning the tyranny of corrupt officials. His retinue arrives and they arrest the corrupt magistrate who is stripped of his position. Yi Mong-ryong rescues Chunhyang and they live happily ever after.

Emergence of books on Hangeul research

By the late Joseon Dynasty, the momentum to research the native Korean language and script had started. People had begun to study dialects and Korean language etymology as well as the principles

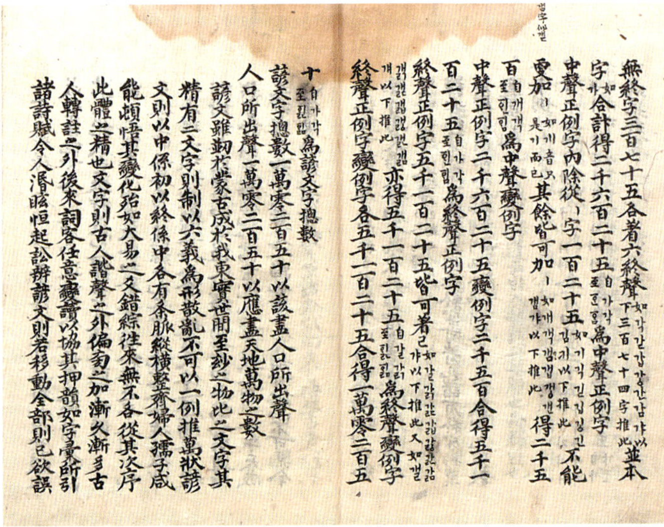
無終字三百七十五各着六終聲並本
字合計得二千六百二十五爲中聲正例字
中聲正例字內除從ㅣ字一百二十五不能
更加ㅣ其餘皆可加ㅣ得二千五
百爲中聲變例字
中聲正例字二千六百二十五變例字二千五百合得五千一
百二十五爲終聲正例字
終聲正例字五千一百二十五皆可着ㄹ亦得五千一百二十五爲終聲變例字
終聲正例字變例字各五千一百二十五合得一萬零二百五
十爲諺文字摠數
諺文字摠數一萬零二百五十以該盡人口所出聲
人口所出聲一萬零二百五十以應盡天地萬物之數
諺文雖刱於蒙古成於我東實世間至玅之物比之文字其
精有二文字則制以六義爲形散亂不可以一例推萬狀諺
文則以中係初以終係中各有条脈縱橫整齊婦人孺子咸
能頓悟其變化殆如大易之爻錯綜往來無不各從其次序
此體之精也文字則古人諧聲之外偏旁之加漸久漸多古
人轉註之外後來詞客任意變讀以協其押韻如字彙所引
諸詩賦令人惛眩恒起訟辨諺文則若移動全部則已欲誤

Eonmunji, a book on Korean language and writing written by Yu Hui, 1824, Kyujanggak Institute for Korean Studies and method behind the creation of Hangeul. The foremost scholars of the time were Sin Gyeong-jun (1712–1781; scholar-official in the reign of Yeongjo of the Silhak, or "practical learning," school) and Yu Hui. Yu Hui was the author of *Eonmunji*, which explores Korean language and writing of the time.

Yu Hui was a late Joseon scholar of the Silhak school who lived from 1773 to 1837. He authored a vast 100-volume work titled *Muntong*, the whereabouts of which is unknown. It was a kind of encyclopedia that reflected his knowledge on many subjects including astronomy, geography, medicine, fortunetelling (with tortoise-shells), horticulture, agricultural management, geomancy (*pungsu*), fish, insects, and birds. He also left behind many valuable texts related to the study of Korean language including *Eonmunji*, *Simul myeonggo* and *Mulmyeong yugo*. *Eonmunji* comprises four parts aside from the preface: examples of initial sounds, examples of medial sounds, examples of final sounds, and a conclusion containing examples of all the Hangeul letters.

Eonmunji established a system of sounds produced by human beings based on a study of Chinese sounds and Korean sounds and then proposed a phonological system for the Korean language at the time. Going beyond the existing methods of study based solely on Chinese-character sounds, this book can be considered the first research attempt to establish a phonology of the Korean language. It is a superlative work that has stood the test of time as its content is equally relevant today. A typeface edition of *Eonmunji* was published in 1938 by the Korean Language Society (Joseoneo Hakhoe), and once again in 1946. *Eonmunji juhae*, an annotated version of the book written by Yu Chang-don, was published in 1958 by Shingu Munhwasa.

Music books and musical scores

In the late Joseon period, court music began to give way to a new genre called *jeong-ak*. *Jeong-ak* was a concept opposite to folk music, its name meaning "music that is graceful, refined and grand." It comprises two categories, vocal music and instrumental music. The poetic song forms *gagok*, *gasa*, and *sijo* all come under the category of vocal music. The major instrumental piece in this genre is "Yeongsanhoesang," which originated in Buddhist music and refers to the Buddha's sermon on Vulture Peak. The major categories of folk music at the time were *pansori*, and *sinawi* and *sanjo*, both of which are improvisational instrumental pieces derived from shaman music.

Akjang gasa: Ballads and Folk Songs

This book contains the lyrics of songs from the late Goryeo period to the early Joseon period and ranges from court music to folk songs. Its compilation is attributed to a man named Park Jun, believed to have lived in the Miryang region sometime between the reigns of King Jungjong and King Myeongjong. It is divided into three parts: lyrics of folk songs, court music lyrics, and other lyrics. It records many Goryeo songs that had only been handed down orally such as "Are You Going?" ("Gasiri"), "Song of the Western Capital" ("Seogyeong byeolgok"), "Dumpling Store" ("Ssanghwajeom"), "Song of the Green Mountain" ("Cheongsan byeolgok"), "Spring Fills the Court" ("Manjeonchun byeolsa"), and "Song of Cheoyong" ("Cheoyong-ga"). *Ballads and Folk Songs (Akjang gasa)* is one of three major music books of Joseon along with *Canon of Music (Akhak gwebeom)* and *Native Music in Contemporary Use (Siyong hyangakbo)*.

Yang geumsinbo: Yang's New Music for the Zither

This musical score for the *geomungo* (six-string zither) compiled by Yang Deok-su in 1610 comprises a woodblock print book of 26 pages. The postscript to the book explains that Yang, a musician, took refuge in Namwon during the Japanese invasions and, with the help of the local magistrate Kim Du-nam, put together this collection of songs for the *geomungo*. Originally the book was meant to be titled *Geumsinbo*, meaning new music for the zither, but the editor's name was added to form the final title *Yang geumsinbo*.

Portrait of King Yeongjo, National Palace Museum of Korea

3. Spread of Hangeul in Everyday Life

Publication of educational texts

Though Yeongjo is the king credited with the revival of Joseon, his path to the throne and his rule was colored with many unsavory incidents. Perhaps for this reason, he left many words of admonition behind for succeeding kings and the people.

Eoje sanghun eonhae: Hangeul translation of advice from the king

To aid the rule of succeeding monarchs, King Yeongjo wrote this book of advice in 1745 (21st year of his reign). It is composed of four main parts: contents, foreword, body and epilogue. The body consists of eight lessons: respect the laws of heaven, uphold the preceding king, build strong ties with relatives, love the people, do not form cliques and take sides, uphold frugality, brace one's spirit, and devote oneself to study.

Each item in this book carries the original Chinese-character text along with the sounds and explanations in Hangeul and a Hangeul translation.

Eoje gyeongmineum: The king's warnings to the people

Published by King Yeongjo in 1762 (38th year of his reign), this book warns the people to always be vigilant. It is a short ten-page text written entirely in Hangeul.

Eoje baekhaengwon: The king's advice on the root of all behavior

This book was written by King Yeongjo in 1765 to encourage the people to practice filial piety. To help the people realize the importance of filial piety and put it into practice, it lists the writings of Confucian sages that can serve as guides. The Chinese characters carry explanations and there is a Hangeul translation attached at the back of the book.

Dialogue between the king and the people

Hangeul flourished in the later Joseon period during the reigns of Yeongjo and Jeongjo, and an especially large number of documents were written in Hangeul during the Jeongjo era. In the case of unfortunate events that affected the lives of the ordinary people, such as a bad harvest or the rampage of a band of thieves, Jeongjo would write messages in Hangeul to the people as a means to placate and control public sentiment.

Royal edict for the people of Gyeonggi-do Province

King Jeongjo wrote a royal edict to the people of Gyeonggi-do Province on the 13th day of the 8th month of 1782. Famine and flooding had caused much suffering that year in the Gyeonggi-do, Chungcheong-do and Gyeongsang-do provinces. But the damage and suffering were particularly bad in Gyeonggi-do, hence the message from the king, part of which is translated into modern language as follows: **20**

To the people of Gyeonggi-do, listen to my thoughts on the matter. According to *Zhouli* [*Rites of Zhou*], of the twelve affairs of state that must be handled in a year of famine, the second is to lighten the tax load. In easing taxes, there is nothing better than lowering rates and decreasing the grain exchange volume.

Royal edict to the people of six provinces

With a bad harvest the following year, in 1783 King Jeongjo wrote another royal edict to the people of Gyeonggi-do, Chungcheong-do, Jeolla-do, Gyeongsang-do, Gangwon-do and Hamgyeong-do provinces. The first birthday of the prince happened to fall in this year, and through this message to the people Jeongjo sought to share the happiness of the occasion and appease and console public sentiment. Part of the edict is translated as follows:

As the first birthday of the prince, this is a joyous day. With heaven overlooking the court, the prince, dressed in his colorful clothes, plays with marbles, giving happiness to his grandmother and mother. How can this be a happy occasion for me alone?

Hangeul and the three bonds and five relationships

From the Confucian perspective, upholding the three bonds and five cardinal relationships was the most important prerequisite for properly establishing the family, society and the nation. After illustrated stories of the three bonds (between king and subject, parents and children, and husband and wife) were published in the early

20. Search of the *Annals of the Joseon Dynasty (Joseon wangjo sillok)* reveals 62 edicts written by King Jeongjo, 26 of which were written in Hangeul.

Joseon period, related books were occasionally published throughout the rest of the dynasty, the most important ones as listed below.

Samgang haengsildo: Illustrated Guide to the Three Bonds

This textbook on morals and ethics for the ordinary people was produced by Seol Sun and other scholars under the command of King Sejong in 1434. It gathers together stories from Chinese and Korean books that exemplify the three bonds. The book comprises three volumes: *Illustration of Filial Piety (Hyojado)*, which highlights 110 famous filial sons; *Illustration of Loyalty (Chungsindo)*, which highlights 112 famously loyal subjects; and *Illustration of Fidelity (Yeolnyeodo)*, which tells the story of 94 chaste and faithful daughters and wives. The Korean figures in these stories include four filial sons, six loyal subjects, and six chaste and faithful women. Each story is illustrated and features Hangeul explanations of the story written above the illustrations and the main text (which is in Chinese characters).

Iryun haengsildo: Illustrated Guide to the Two Relationships

This book contains stories of people who exemplify two of the five relationships: the etiquette required in relationships with people older than oneself, and the trust required in relationships with friends. The people represented are 48 famous sages from China. This book was compiled by Jo Gwang-jo and others under the command of King Jungjong, who sought to bring society back to normal after the misery brought about by the former ruler Yeonsangun. With the book the king sought to establish ethical norms and edify the people.

Oryun haengsildo: Illustrated Guide to the Five Relationships

Under the command of King Jeongjo, Yi Byeong-mo and other

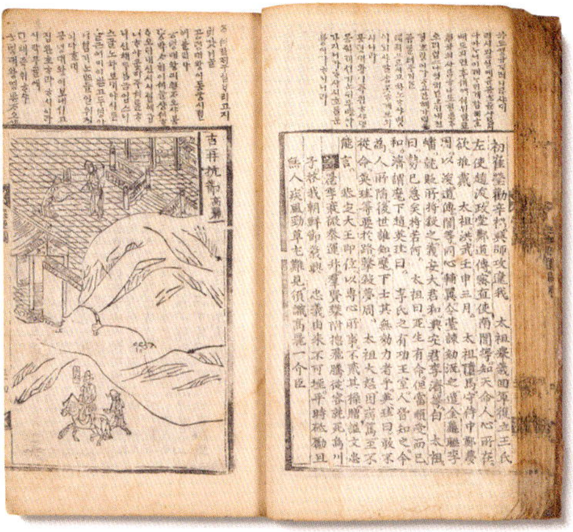

Samgang haengsildo (Illustrated Guide to the Three Bonds).
National Museum of Korea

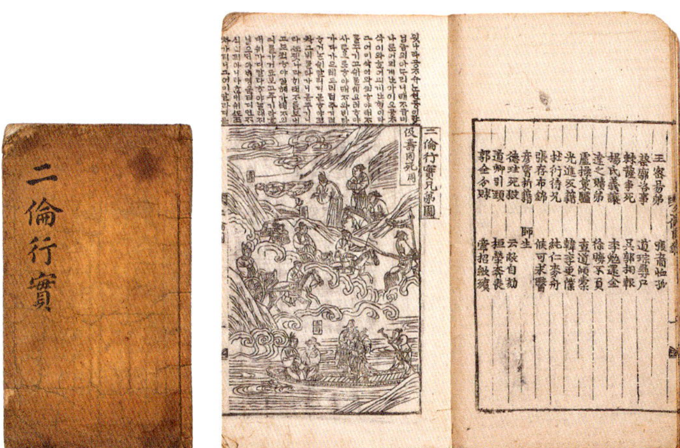

Iryun haengsildo (Illustrated Guide to the Two Relationships), National Museum of Korea scholars published this book in 1797 by combining the two existing books mentioned above, that on the three bonds (*Samgang haengsildo*) and that on the two relationships (*Iryun haengsildo*). The foreword of this combined work contains King Jeongjo's explanation for publication of the book: "The preceding books on the three bonds and the two relationships were published one after the other and distributed to schools, thus providing a foundation for encouraging good customs and influencing the people for good." The illustrations are accompanied by written stories in Chinese characters as well as a Hangeul translation.

Hangeul and the education of women

All the educational institutions established by the state from the Three Kingdoms period to the Joseon Dynasty were for men only. It was thought that a woman should look after the home and cultivate the necessary character, qualities and virtues to become a faithful wife and devoted mother. One of the most important virtues was the ability to cook, and from the mid-Joseon period cookbooks written in Hangeul began to circulate. This attests to the spread of Hangeul among the ordinary people and its impact on aspects of everyday life and rites of passage.

Naehun: Instructions for Women

This book was compiled in 1475 by Queen Sohye, the mother of King Seongjong, to instruct women. It is a collection of excerpts from Confucian writings of China including the *Biographies of Exemplary Women (Lienu zhuan)*, *Lesser Learning (Xiao xue)*, *Lessons for Women (Nujiao)*, and the Korean compilation *Myeonggam (Clear Mirror)*. The first chapter "Speech and Behavior" (Eonhaeng) contains warnings

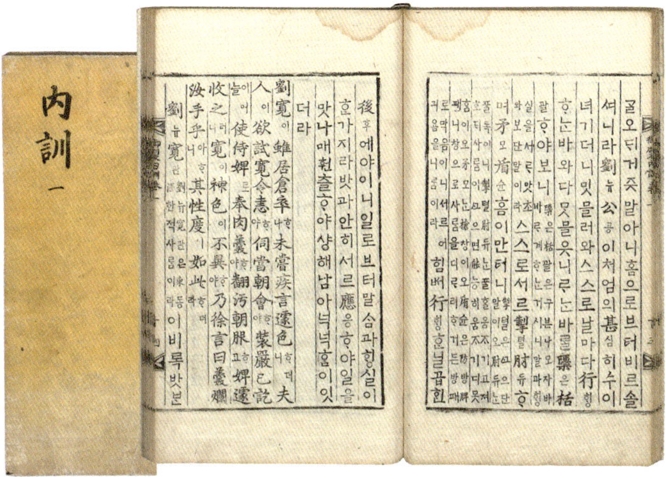

Naehun (Instructions for Women). Kyujanggak Institute for Korean Studies

regarding proper speech and behavior; the second chapter "Filial Piety" (Hyochin) gives instructions on how to treat parents with proper respect; the third chapter "Marriage" (Hollye) prescribes the proper wedding etiquette; chapter four "Husband and Wife" (Bubu) prescribes the duties of a married couple; chapter five "Maternal Duties" (Moui) prescribes the etiquette for mothers; chapter six "Good Relations" (Donmok) describes how to maintain good relations with relatives; and chapter seven "Yeonggeom" is a guide to clean and thrifty housekeeping, how to treat guests, and how to look after one's husband.

Eumsik dimibang: Gourmet Recipes

This cookbook was written by Lady Jang (1598–1680) of the

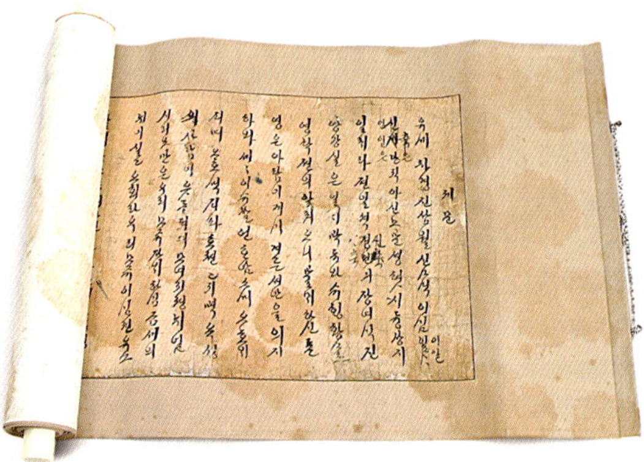

Ritual paper written in the court script style (*gungche*). Central Museum of Kyunghee University

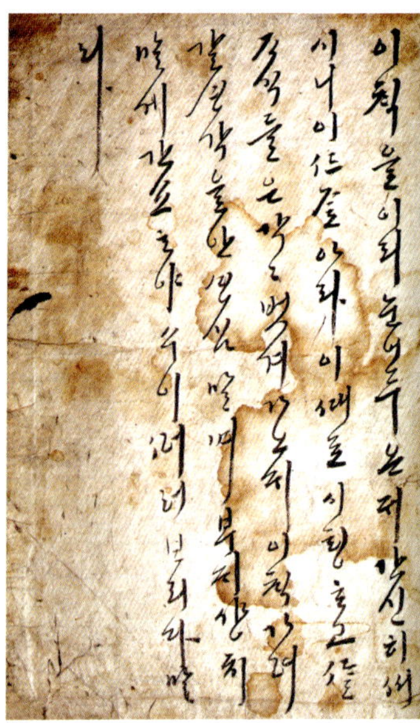

Eumsik dimibang* *(Gourmet Recipes)
Source: Andong Cultural Resource Portal

Andong Jang clan in her later years as a way to pass down the family recipes to her daughters and daughters-in-law. Containing the recipes of 146 dishes, it is the oldest Korean cookbook written in Hangeul. The recipes include 18 for noodles, rice cakes and dumplings; 74 for fish and meat dishes, and 54 for liquor and vinegar. An additional section titled "Matjil bangmun" (Recipes from the Village of Matjil) contains the recipes for 16 dishes prepared in the way of Lady Jang's maternal relatives of the Andong Jang clan. The following warning is included at the end of the book.

> As my eyes are failing, I have barely managed to complete this book. Keeping this in mind, follow the recipes as they are written. Daughters of the family should copy the recipes, but do not dream of taking the book. Make sure it is well preserved and kept from damage. Do not let it fall apart too quickly.

Gyuhap chongseo: Handbook for Women

This book is a kind of encyclopedia on matters related to food, clothing and shelter, or housekeeping in general, written by Lady Yi Bingheogak in 1809 during the early half of the reign of King Sunjo. It is composed of five chapters: "Jusaui," dealing with the way to make *jang* (red pepper paste and soybean paste), liquor, rice and rice cakes, and various side dishes; "Bongimchick," dealing with sericulture, weaving, dyeing, embroidery, and clothes making; "Sangarak," dealing with cultivating the fields, caring for flowers and bamboo, and raising livestock; "Cheongnanggyeol," dealing with family health matters such as child rearing methods and first aid; and "Sulsuryak," dealing with fortunetelling according to the orientation of a house, driving away evil spirits, and how to avoid being deceived by shamans.

Ⅳ. Reform and Challenges in the Use of Written and Spoken Language

Joseon was called on to seek a new model for society and new values in the wake of two wars, the Japanese invasions of Korea in 1592-1598 and the second Manchu invasion of 1636. The whole country was overrun by Japan, which had adopted Western culture before Joseon; King Injo surrendered to the Manchus, who had founded the Qing Dynasty and newly emerged as a powerful force in the region, and Crown Prince Sohyeon was taken hostage; and the Ming Dynasty, the then suzerain state of Joseon, was conquered by the Manchus. Joseon was forced to honor the Qing Dynasty as its new suzerain state, but the Qing Dynasty itself was also emasculated by Western forces.

In this process, the efforts of kings Yeongjo and Jeongjo seemed to bring a new renaissance for Joseon but were not enough to restore the nation, whose fortunes had been already begun to decline. Joseon had to make the bold choice of either introducing or boycotting Western Learning, or establishing a whole new system of values. Either way required smooth communication between the government and the ordinary people, which led to the popularization of Hangeul.

1. Internal and External Circumstances in Late Joseon
2. Drastic Changes in Literacy in Daily Life
3. Fall of the Nation and Crisis of Hangeul

The calligraphy of King Cheoljong, National Museum of Korea

lowing year, three French naval ships led by Admiral Cecile arrived at the shores of Chungcheong-do Province. A Western ship of unknown nationality was seen again off the coast of Hamgyeong-do Province in 1848. Despite such frequent appearance of foreign ships, Joseon stubbornly held fast to its closed-door policy. However, after two attacks, the French Disturbance of 1866 and the American Disturbance of 1871, Joseon was forced by Japan to sign the Korea-Japan Treaty of 1876 (also known as the Treaty of Ganghwa) and open its doors.

Decline of China

Although the Qing Dynasty, suzerain state of Joseon, introduced Western culture before Joseon, it failed in modern reform and began to fall into ruin. In addition, the Chinese dynasty was unable to withstand Western invasions, and in 1842 it signed the Treaty of Nanking, which gave Britain sovereignty over Hong Kong and forced Qing to open five ports – Guangdong, Xiamen, Shanghai, Fuzhou, and Ningbo. Moreover, Qing had to pay an indemnity equal to about $18 million. Accordingly, the Qing Dynasty had by this time lost all power as a suzerain state.

In 1860, the Qing Dynasty lost a war against French-British allied forces that had captured Tianjin and Beijing and was forced to sign the Treaty of Peking (Beijing) with Britain and France. Under the treaty, China handed over Kowloon and was compelled to open another nine ports including Tianjin, Wumen, Shantou, Wujiang, Jibu, Hangu, Jinjiang, Qiongzhou, and Jiujiang. In addition, it was to guarantee free propagation of Western religion, allow Western diplomatic ministers to be stationed in Beijing, and on top of that pay another indemnity. Such circumstances in China forced Joseon to seek a breakthrough in its external relations.

Qing Dynasty Soldiers, 18th century, National Museum of Korea

Introduction of Western Learning

By this time, Western Learning (Catholicism) had entered Joseon and its propagation had begun. In response, an indigenous relgion called Donghak, or Eastern Learning, rose up and gained a big following among the commoners. As a way to facilitate the spread of their beliefs and reach as many people as possible both the Western Learning and Eastern Learning camps published their own sacred books – for example, *The Song of Heaven (Cheonju gasa)* and *Hymns from the Dragon Pool (Yongdam yusa)* – written in Hangeul, which had been held in contempt. This paved the way for Hangeul to rapidly spread among the public.

Exposure to Western Learning and Catholicism

In 1601, Matteo Ricci (1552–1610), an Italian priest working in Beijing, China, introduced Western Learning and culture while propagating Roman Catholicism among the Chinese. He also served as a conduit of Chinese culture to the Western world.

The Western world became known to the people of Joseon when some Koreans brought back from Beijing a range of Catholic scriptures and science books. At the time, Joseon's Confucian scholars learned about Catholicism from *True Principles of Catholicism* written by Matteo Ricci. The book was first introduced to Joseon by Yi Sugwang, a Neo-Confucian scholar who actively advocated the introduction of Western Learning and the culture of the Qing Dynasty. Later, Crown Prince Sohyeon, who had been taken hostage during the Manchu Invasion of 1636, began to learn about Catholicism and the scientific knowledge of the West when he met the German priest Adam Schall.

Catholicism became widely known in Joseon in 1784 when Yi

Seung-hun, baptized in Beijing, returned to Joseon and began propagating the new religion. Confucian scholars approached Catholicism with an academic interest and then gradually accepted it as a religious belief. Such a transition was regarded as contradictory to the laws and systems and customs of Joseon and thus a factor promoting social discord. This suggests the emergence of new forces seeking to reform the entire social structure and value system.

A couple of societal characteristics of Joseon can be inferred from the acceptance of Catholicism and the demand for social reform: First, Joseon, already in a serious state of decline, had reached the point of collapse in its social structure. Second, the spread of Catholicism and Western Learning was strongest among the ruling literati class of Joseon. In other words, introduction of Catholic doctrines and Western Learning came about not because of Western missionaries or outside forces but the intellectual curiosity and deliberate efforts of Joseon intellects.

Spread of Hangeul through Catholicism

During the 1880s, the shift from a closed-door policy to an open-door policy brought about radical changes in all aspects of Joseon, including its politics, economy, society, and culture. In particular, the traditional Confucian education was replaced by new education based on modern sciences.

The Catholic Church built schools to provide Koreans with modern education. In 1882, a school with 11 students was founded in Inhyeon-dong, Seoul, which was the forerunner of Gyeseong Elementary School. In 1883, the Catholic Church founded a college chinois named Hanhan Hagwon where Hangeul and Chinese characters were taught together, along with other subjects intended for enlightenment of the people. By 1893, there were 38 Catholic schools

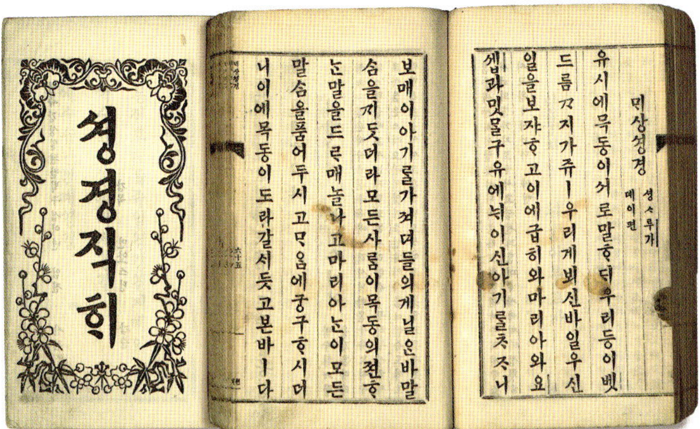

Literal Translation of the Bible, 1897, Printed with metal type. Korean Publishers Association

across the country with 376 students. Eleven years later, in 1904 the numbers had increased to 75 schools and 693 students. With such expansion, the Catholic Church, based on the principle of sexual equality, strove to eradicate paternalism and the idea of predominance of men over women, the traditional values of Confucianism which prevailed in Joseon. In this respect, it placed much emphasis on the education of women. Catholic schools not only taught female students things helpful for everyday life such as sewing, cleaning, laundering, childrearing, embroidery, and silk weaving but also Hangeul, Chinese characters, arithmetic, history, and geography. Such education greatly contributed to the dissemination of Hangeul among the public.

From the beginning of its introduction to Joseon, Catholicism contributed considerably to the advancement of Hangeul. The manuscript of the "Song of the Ten Commandments," Korea's first *cheonju gasa* (doctrinal teachings in traditional poetic song form) written in Hangeul, is contained in *Mancheon yugo*, the posthumous works of Yi Seung-hun. The footnote attached to the song reads: "The lyrics were written by Jeong Yak-jeon, Gwon Sang-hak, and Yi Chong-eok after their delivering a lecture at Jueosa Temple in December 1779." This suggests that the "Song of the Ten Commandments" was the joint effort of the three scholars. Around the same time, "Song in Praise of God" was also composed by Yi Byeok, which suggests that Hangeul was already in wide use among Catholics in Joseon.

In the late 1790s, *Essentials of the Lord's Teaching*, a catechism in Hangeul written by Jeong Yak-jong, was also published, further contributing to the spread of Hangeul. In this early stage when there was no Korean Bible, the Hangeul catechism served as a kind of replacement. Later, the Gospel of Luke and the Gospel of John were translated into Korean in the 1880s.

It can be said that the Roman Catholic Church played a significant role in disseminating Hangeul through the foundation of schools where Hangeul was taught and the publication of Catholic catechisms. Such activities, though intended to spread Catholic doctrines, nevertheless greatly contributed to development of the Korean language and script and the eradication of illiteracy.

Founding of Donghak

Donghak is a native religion founded in April 1860 by Choe Je-u. Based on worship of the Lord of Heaven (*cheonju*), its doctrines were to protect Joseon from foreign forces and ensure the wellbeing of the ordinary people. Donghak appeared around the same time Western Learning was introduced through Catholicism and spread throughout Joseon. The name Donghak, meaning "Eastern Learning," was a

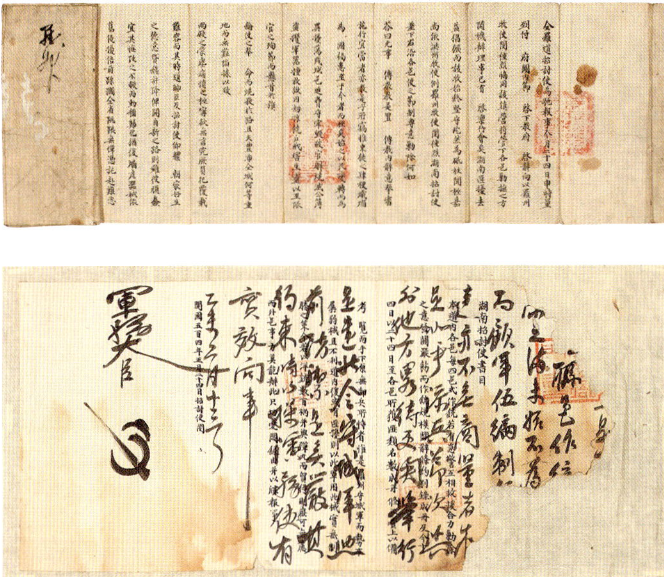

A report on the status of the Donghak Peasant Revolution submitted by the Honam Chotosa (official in charge of putting down the rebellion), National Museum of Korea

counter response to the introduction of Seohak, or Western Learning. Donghak hence has characteristics of both nationalist and social movements. In 1905, Son Byeong-hui changed the name of the religion to Cheondogyo, or Religion of the Heavenly Way.

At the time of its foundation, Joseon confronted difficulties inside and outside the nation. Externally, Joseon fought the encroaching Western Learning and culture. Internally, traditional Confucian values declined and government was rife with corrupt officials. Donghak was a religion based on worship of "Hanul," or the "Lord of Heaven," and upheld the idea that individuals could be agents for promoting national interests and ensuring the welfare of the people. The main religious doctrine advocated by Choe Si-hyeong, the second leader of Donghak, was "serve man as God," which later developed into the idea that "man is God" under the third leader, Son Byeong-hui.

In late Joseon, the ruling *yangban* class began to fall apart, and the significance of Donghak lies in the leading role taken by the peasants who comprised the working class or lower class of society in its propagation, though they were unfamiliar with reading and writing. In other words, Donghak as a religion and the Eastern Learning movement constituted a social reform movement against the dynastic society, a movement not led by the ruling class or the royal family but by the marginalized commoners.

The Donghak Peasant Uprising of 1894 (31st year of King Gojong) developed into a social reform movement under the idea that everybody is equal. After Donghak was renamed Cheondogyo in 1905, it continued to participate in enlightenment of the public. Indeed, Cheondogyo greatly contributed to the new education movement in Korea through operation of schools such as Boseong School[21] and Dongdeok School.[22] These schools taught "Korean language" as a separate subject and played a leading role in disseminating Hangeul, the Korean script.

Yongdam yusa: Hymns from the Dragon Pool

The close correlation between the development of Donghak and the dissemination of Hangeul is evidenced by *Hymns from the Dragon*

21. Boseong School was a private school founded by Yi Yong-ik in August 1906. The Cheondogyo leader Son Byeong-hui took over control of the school in 1910.
22. Dongdeok School was Korea's first private girls' school founded by a civilian in 1908.

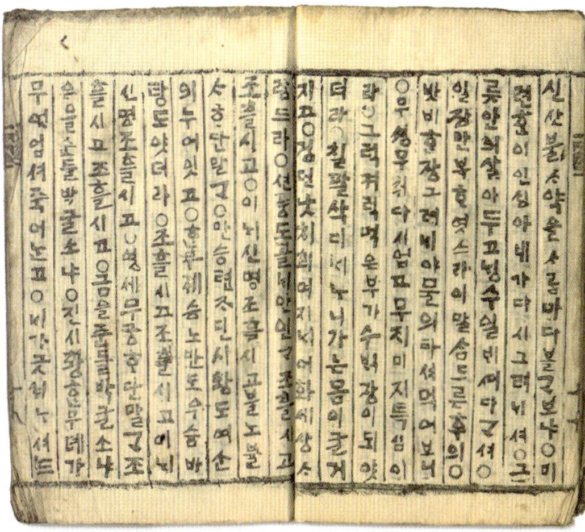

Yongdam yusa (Hymns from the Dragon Pool). Late 1800s. Woodblock print. Bumwoosa Publishing Co.

Pool (Yongdam yusa), a Donghak scripture which was written in Hangeul. As the basic scripture of Donghak along with *Great Eastern Scripture (Donggyeong daejeon)* written in Chinese, *Hymns from the Dragon Pool* was written in Hangeul by Choe Je-u between 1860 and 1863 in the form of *gasa*. It includes a collection of nine Hangeul *gasa* such as "Song of the Dragon Pool," "Song of Consolation," "Song of Urging Study." Like Western Learning, Donghak was targeted to the commoner class of Joseon, including the peasants, and for this reason, the scripture was published in the form of Hangeul *gasa*. But whatever the reason for using Hangeul, it can be presumed that the growth of Donghak also meant the penetration of Hangeul into the everyday life of the ordinary people of Joseon.

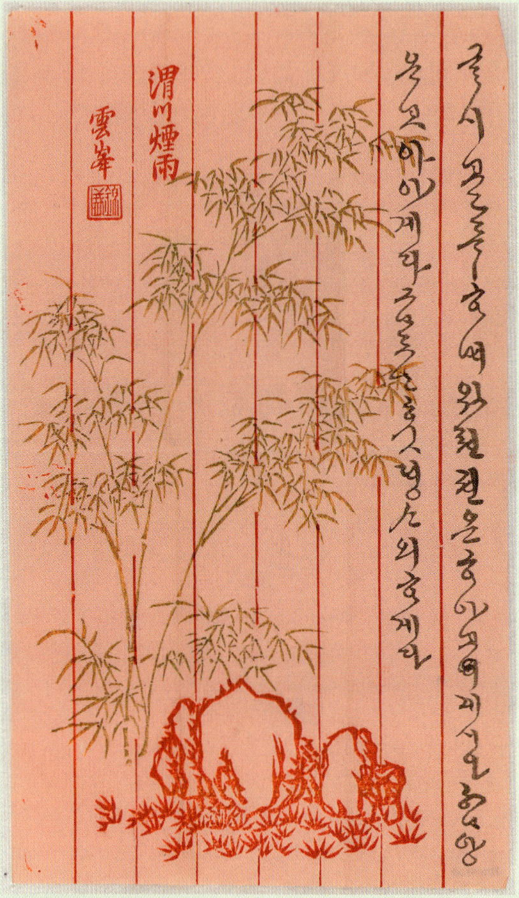

Letter written in Hangeul by Empress Myeongseong, National Palace Museum of Korea

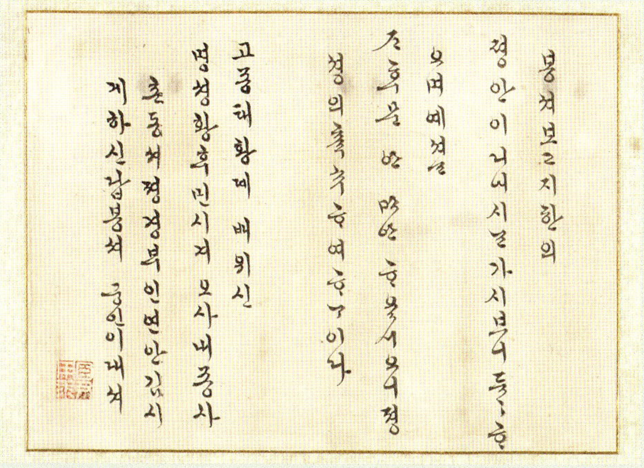

Sealed letter written by Empress Myeongseong.
National Palace Museum of Korea

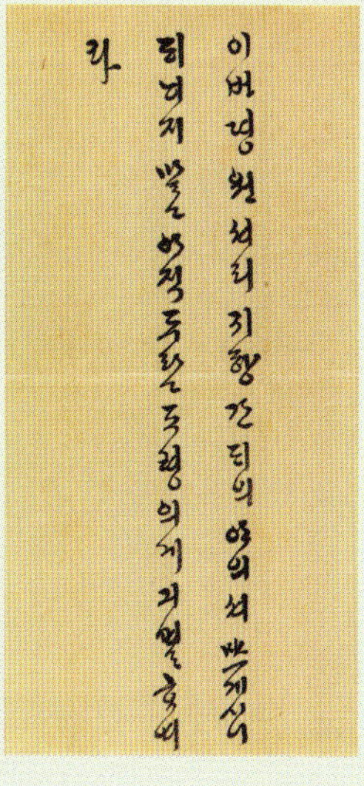

Letter written in Hangeul by a court lady.
National Palace Museum of Korea

2. Drastic Changes in Literacy in Daily Life

Hangeul-centered literacy

Joseon signed pacts with foreign countries and opened its doors to them in the 1870s. As a result, there was a rush of foreign cultures and institutions into the country and attempts were made to build a new society modeled on the imported cultures and institutions.

Chief among such efforts were the advent of the press and distribution of newspapers among the public and the establishment of modern school education. Founded in 1886, the *Hanseong Jubo* (Hanseong Weekly Bulletin) published articles in a mix of Hangeul and Chinese characters. Following the Gabo Reforms of 1894, this mixture of Hangeul and Chinese characters became the norm, even in official government documents and gazettes. *Elementary Reader for Citizens*, the elementary school Korean textbook published in 1895, also used Hangeul along with Chinese characters while middle school textbooks published after 1895 mostly used Korean. The *Independent*, a government-supported newspaper inaugurated in 1896 by Seo Jae-pil, was published only in Hangeul.

Policy shifted from the use of Chinese characters and Idu for official government documents to the use of Hangeul and Chinese characters. Meanwhile, some private organizations used only Hangeul,

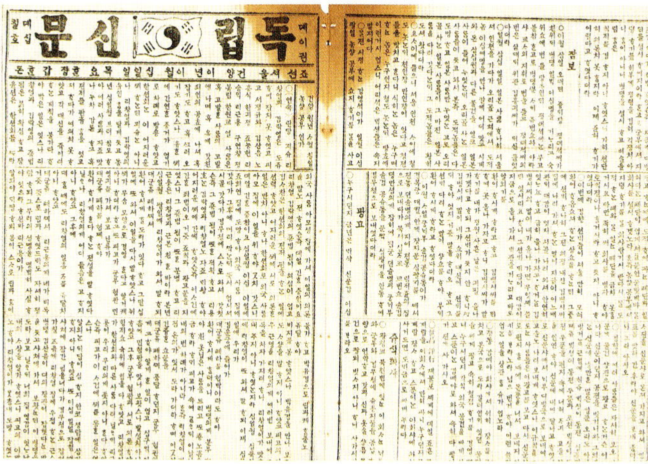

독립신문

The ***Independent***, National Museum of Korea

which revolutionized reading and writing for Koreans.

The *Independent*

The *Independent* was Korea's first modern newspaper, privately published on April 7, 1986. Seo Jae-pil and Ju Si-gyeong who ran the newspaper used Hangeul exclusively and instituted word spacing. Such moves had a decisive effect on the writing system used by various private newspapers that began to appear at the end of the Daehan Empire. However, the *Independent* came under government repression due to its revolutionary and enlightening tone and finally ceased publication with its final edition on December 4, 1899. April 7, which is observed as Newspaper Day every year, marks the date the *Independent* was first issued.

New novels

The "new novel" refers to works of fiction that appeared between the late 19th and the early 20th centuries. Their emergence can be attributed to changes in the way of life driven by the Gabo Reforms and the Donghak Peasant Uprising of 1894, a secure readership among the middle-class women, increased space for publication due to the appearance of privately owned newspapers, the buildup of inherent tradition, and the influence of imported foreign literature. The new novels mainly dealt with themes such as reform of political and social institutions, reform of customs, new ideas on education, the liberation of women and their social and cultural equality, and a scientific view of the world. The considerable effect the new novels had on the dissemination of Hangeul is shown in the following passage.

> *Seoyu gyeonmun (Travelogue to the West)* by Yu Gil-jun published in 1895, newspapers, and translated materials used Hangeul along with Chinese characters, which played a decisive role in implementing a campaign for exclusive use of the Korean language and expanding readership.
>
> In particular, newspapers published at the time played a pioneering role in introducing the mixed use of Hangeul and Chinese characters, contributing to the spread of Hangeul among the public, coupled with new novels printed in these newspapers including *Hyeolui nu (Tears of Blood)*, written by Yi In-jik, which was published in the *Mansebo Daily*. Consequently, the sentences produced in a mix of Hangeul and Chinese characters, and the newspapers and new novels which featured such sentence, were closely connected as mediums for communication and the dissemination of new culture. There was also a close connection between readers of newspapers and new novels.

However, the most immediate factor behind the emergence of new novels is the Koreans' strong desire to share the new cultures and knowledge imported at that time.

Publication of Korean language textbooks

Under the new educational system brought by the Gabo Reforms of 1894, it was necessary to establish new subjects and create the contents to go with them. In village schools called *seodang*, a major educational institution before modern schools, students were given Chinese-centered education including the *Thousand Character Classic*, the Confucian classics, and historical records. This system made it impossible to provide independent national education or to teach practical courses such as science, mathematics, and business.

To break away from education based on literary Chinese and enhance national prosperity and defense through new learning, it was necessary to renew awareness of Korean culture and improve the writing system as a prerequisite for new learning. To that end, the first thing to do was to publish a Korean language textbook. So in 1895, the Ministry of Education published the *Elementary Reader for Citizens*, which used Hangeul along with Chinese as shown in the following passage:

> 우리大朝鮮은 亞細亞洲中의一王國이라… 吾等은如此ᄒᆞᆫ나라에生ᄒᆞ야今日에와셔 世界萬國과修好通商ᄒᆞ야富强을닷토ᄂᆞᆫ셰에當ᄒᆞ얏시니…

As the contents of this textbook were difficult for beginners, however, and did not meet the needs of that time, private schools founded afterwards published their own textbooks that were designed to instill students with national pride and an independent spirit.

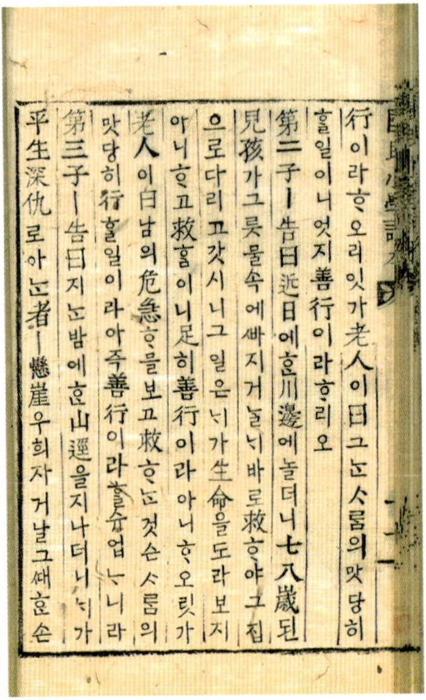

行이라ᄒᆞ오리잇가老人이曰그ᄂᆞᆫᄉᆞᄅᆞᆷ의맛당히
ᄒᆞᆯ일이니엇지善行이라ᄒᆞ리오
第二子ㅣ告曰近日에ᄒᆞᆫ川邊에놀더니七八歲된
見孩가그릇물속에ᄲᅡ지거ᄂᆞᆯᄂᆡ바로救ᄒᆞ야그집
으로다리고갓시니그일은ᄂᆡ가生命을도라보지
아니ᄒᆞ고救ᄒᆞᆷ이니足히善行이라아니ᄒᆞ오릿가
老人이曰남의危急ᄒᆞᆷ을보고救ᄒᆞᄂᆞᆫ것슨ᄉᆞᄅᆞᆷ의
맛당히行ᄒᆞᆯ일이라아주善行이라ᄒᆞᆯ슈업ᄂᆞ니라
第三子ㅣ告曰지ᄂᆞᆫ밤에ᄒᆞᆫ山逕을지나더니ᄂᆡ가
平生深仇로아ᄂᆞᆫ者ㅣ懸崖우희자거ᄂᆞᆯ그때ᄒᆞᆫ손

Elementary Reader for Citizens, 1895, Printed with wooden type, Bumwoosa Publishing Co.

But following the Protectorate Treaty of 1905, the Ministry of Education under the Japanese government deleted all contents encouraging Koreans' national and independent consciousness from the existing textbook and published a new one titled the *Korean Reader (Gugeo dokbon)*.

Volume one of this textbook is composed of forty-five chapters: the introduction shows Hangeul vowels and consonants in order; chapters one to seven contain pictures of objects and their respective names in Hangeul as a learning exercise; chapters eight to eleven guide students through simple words and phrases. From chapter twelve, students begin to learn short sentences for the study of composition; chapter forty-five introduces fairly long sentences, and the final chapter introduces the composition of Hangeul syllables. The book is written only in Hangeul, but the orthography is quite different from what it is today, as shown in the following example from chapter twenty-three (line divisions and spacing are shown as they are in the original):

> 란쵸도향긔가됴타。
> 란쵸쏫츤ᄌᆞ지빗치다。
> 파쵸입흔크기가키갓다。
> 소나무ᄂᆞᆫ뎡ᄌᆞ갓다。
> 바들가지ᄂᆞᆫ느러젓다。

Under such circumstances, the first task for those involved in Korean language education and concerned with the nation's future was to make writing consistent with speech and standardize orthography. Korean intellectuals of the day believed that the national identity could be established through reform of the written and the spoken language, and that this must be preceded by identification of the nature of the Korean language.

Modification of orthographic rules

The start of grammar research

Along with the attempt to organize the orthographical rules for practical purposes, the work of writing down the Korean grammar[23] began as part of the effort to identify the nature of the Korean language. The work of systemizing Korean grammar was initially conducted for the sake of the national language policy and Korean language education. Later, the focus shifted to the description of Korean linguistics. Study of Korean linguistics during this period is particular important in the history of Korean linguistics because it provided a wider perspective on the Korean language and laid the groundwork for the study of traditional grammar.

Korean Grammar (Joseon munjeon) written by Yu Gil-jun is widely regarded as the first Korean grammar book and mainly deals with the theories of sentences and syntax. *Grammar of the National Language (Gugeo munbeop)*, written by Ju Si-gyeong and published in 1910, is a comprehensive Korean grammar book that deals with phonology (letters), morphology (word class), and syntax. Such description of Korean grammar by dividing it into the three parts is now well established as the tradition for Korean grammar books.

"New Edition of the National Writing" by Ji Seok-yeong

Ji Seok-yeong, dean of Korea's first government-funded medical school and the first Korean to administer vaccinations, drafted a radical, unified spelling system that proposed elimination of the widely used vowel • and creation of the new vowel = in its place. The draft was submitted to King Gojong by Sim Sang-hun, the then Deputy Prime Minister, and Min Yeong-cheol, the Minister of Education. It was approved on July 19, 1905, and promulgated under the name "New Edition of the National Writing."

However, implementation of the new spelling system drawn up by an individual without expert review sparked strong opposition from intellectuals. As the situation evolved to the point where Lee

23. Korean grammar refers to rules related to phonemes, syntax, and the lexicon of the Korean language. The scope of the subject of Korean grammar varies, depending on the level of development of Korean linguistics and changes in public awareness of the national language.

Official seal of the Ministry of Education, Daehan Empire, National Museum of Korea

Neung-hwa submitted a new draft titled "Suggestions for a Unified Spelling System" in 1906, the government established the National Language Research Institute (under the Ministry of Education) to address such issues.

National Language Research Institute

The National Language Research Institute was established as a Hangeul research center by the Ministry of Education of the Daehan Empire in 1907 in order to standardize Korean orthographic rules. The establishment of this research institute is mentioned in the forepart of a report on the standardization for Korean orthographic rules.

The research institute was established by approval of the king as an affiliate to the Ministry of Education in 1907. The idea for its creation was first put forth by Minster of Education Lee Jae-gon during a cabinet meeting and the draft proposal was passed. Afterwards the then Prime Minster Lee Wan-yong and Minster of Education Lee Jae-gon submitted it to the king.

The research institute was at that time staffed with nine employees. The report states that there were three Japanese including an assistant administrator and a clerk, and six Korean researchers. The report also says that the research institute was in operation for three years, during which time 23 meetings were held.

The research center began operation on September 16, 1907 and closed on December 27, 1909. In the first year, five meetings were held; in the second year twelve, and in the third year six.

The National Language Research Institute aimed to carry out research on the basic rules and history of the Korean language, and its current usage and recommendations for improvement. In relation to the use of Korean, the ten most worthwhile research tasks were proposed as follows:

1. To identify the origin of Hangeul and the history of Hangeul and its pronunciation
2. To determine whether initial sounds such as ㆁ, ㆆ, ㅿ, ◇, ㅱ, ㅸ, ㆄ, ㅹ are to be used
3. To determine whether tense sounds among initial sounds shall be written as ㄲ, ㄸ, ㅃ, ㅆ, ㅉ, ㆅ
4. To decide on the removal of the vowel sound ㆍ and the cre-

ation of the new vowel sound =

5. To determine the usage of final consonants ㄷ, ㅅ and on the common use of six consonants ㅈ, ㅊ, ㅋ, ㅌ, ㅍ, ㅎ as final consonants
6. To settle the problem of differentiation between seven letters and whether they are clear or muddy (unvoiced or voiced) sounds
7. To decide on the use of the four tones chart and the notation of pitch changes
8. To designate the names of each consonant and vowel of the Korean script
9. To determine the sequential arrangement of letters and lines
10. To standardize Korean orthographic rules

Those who had participated in research of these tasks at the National Language Research Institute gathered their opinions and submitted a report on the standardization for Korean orthographic rules. As Korea's national power declined, however, the research institute was unable to properly fulfill its role.

Korean Orthographic Rules for Elementary School (announced April 1912)

Right after the Japanese annexation of Korea, the Government-General enacted or amended the Korean orthographic rules on three separate occasions. The Education Bureau appointed committee members and held a series of meetings for five months from July through November 1911 before it announced the Korean orthographic rules for school education, the second set of rules to be announced after the "New Edition of the National Writing" by Ji Seok-yeong and the first rules to be announced with the consensus of

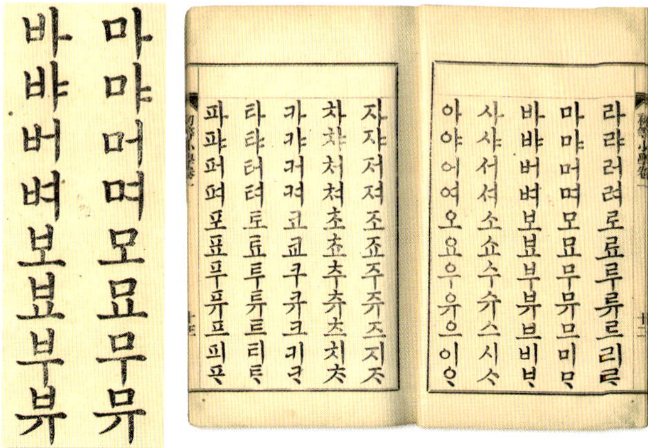

Korean Language Textbook for Elementary School, Volume 1, 1907, Printed with metal type, Korean Publishers Association

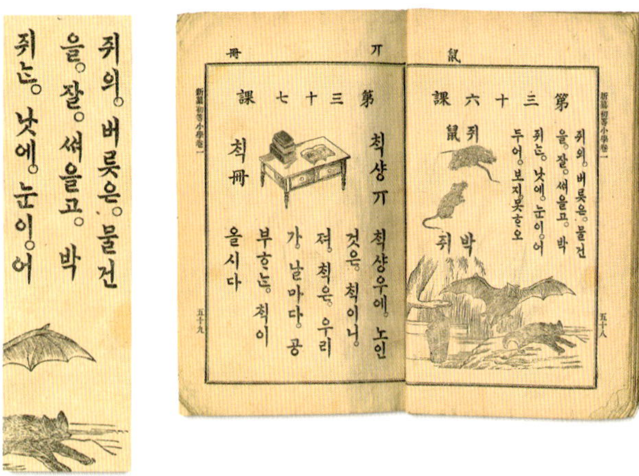

New Edition of the Korean Language Textbook for Elementary School, Volume 1, 1909, Printed with metal type, Samseong Museum of Publishing

scholars. The rules stipulated that first, Seoul speech shall be used as standard Korean; second, modern spelling rules shall be preferred to the historical rules; and third, phonetic representations shall be observed. These rules served as Korea's first general spelling guidelines.

Consequently, based on the vernacular used in Seoul, the vowel sound ㆍ was eliminated from the vowel repertoire for representation of Korean native words, and writing of the syllables 댜, 뎌, 됴, 듀 was changed to 자, 저, 조, 주. However, in respect to the representation of Chinese-character sounds, historical orthography was chosen, which meant 댜, 뎌, 됴, 듀 remained unchanged, and the transcription rules for tense sounds, including the double consonants ㅼ, ㅺ, ㅽ were also maintained according to common usage. Since the distinction between the phonetic representation principle and the division of lexical and grammatical morphemes was vague, the notation of both seven final consonants and syllabication were, in turn, a little confusing.

The situation being such, the necessity of revising the ill-designed Korean orthographic rules was discussed. In response, the Education Bureau reappointed committee members and declared a new Korean spelling system in a report titled "Summary of the Korean Orthographic Rules for Elementary School" in March 1921. However, in substance the new rules were almost identical to those announced in 1912, apart from the newly raised issue of whether to use other symbols as final consonants besides the existing seven.

Korean orthographic rules

Almost a decade later in February 1930, the Education Bureau promulgated the "Rules of Korean Orthography" after deliberation by the committee on the two separate occasions. The first deliberation session was held between September 1928 and January 1929 and the second from May to July 1929.

The newly announced rules stressed that the first and second principles stipulated in its predecessor should be strictly followed: first, Seoul speech shall be used as standard Korean; and second, modern spelling rules shall be preferred to the historical rules. However, the new rules abolished the third principle on the observance of phoneticism.

As a result, aside from several final consonants such as ㅋ, ㅎ, ㅆ other final consonants were to be expressed according to the current spelling rules, and Chinese-character sounds were to be written as they were pronounced in Korean instead of following historical orthographic principles. In particular, the rules for representation of tense sounds, which had been at the center of controversy in the academic circle at the time, were changed so that ㅅ was not laterally attached to different consonants but the same consonant was repeated as shown in the representation of double consonant sounds ㄲ, ㄸ, ㅃ, ㅆ, ㅉ.

As a result, the "Rules of Korean Orthography" announced by the Government-General of Korea are almost identical to the "Proposal for Unified Korean Orthography" that came out several years later. Scholars who played a pivotal role in the establishment of the later proposal had also been involved in establishment of the "Rules of Korean Orthography." As stated in the record of its amendment, the "Rules of Korean Orthography" was designed to standardize spelling rules widely used by the public at the time. This same goal was also reflected in the "Proposal for Unified Korean Orthography."

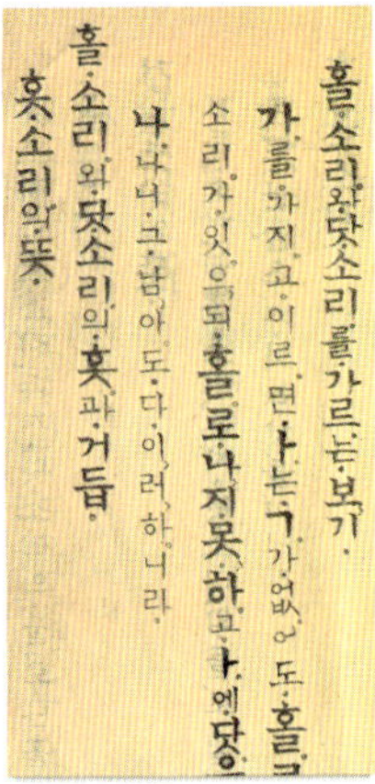

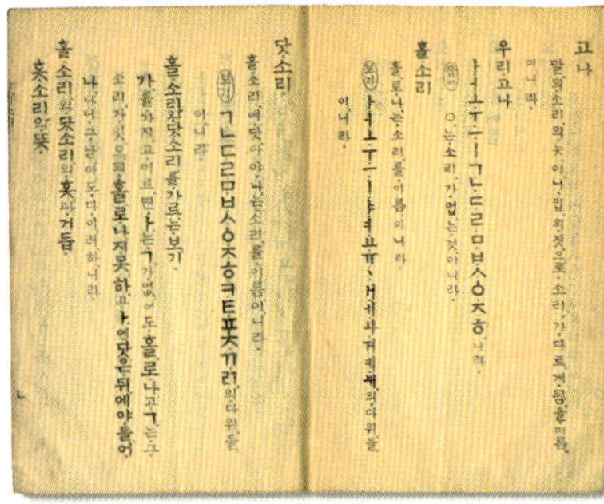

The Sounds of Speech written by Ju Si-gyeong, 1914, Lithographic print, Bumwoosa Publishing Co.

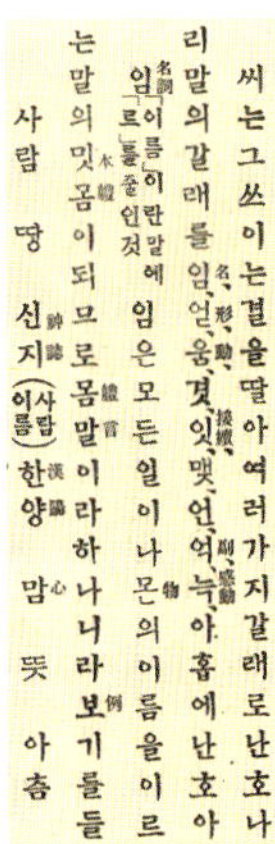

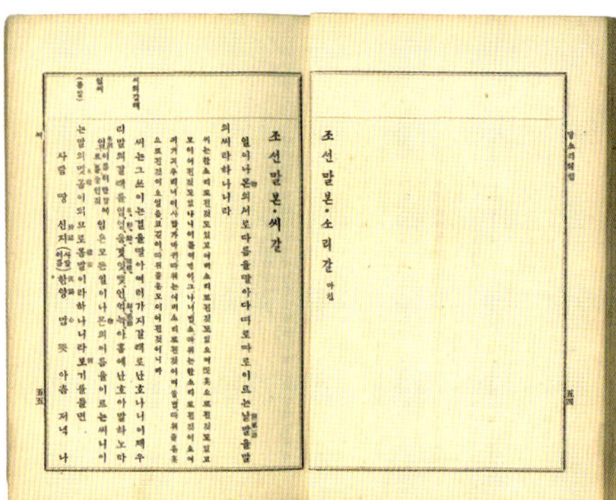

Joseon malbon, a Korean language grammar book written by Kim Du-bong, 1916, Printed with metal type, Bumwoosa Publishing Co.

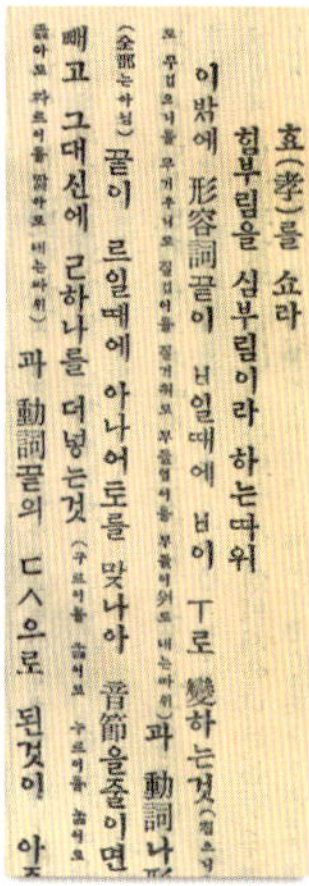

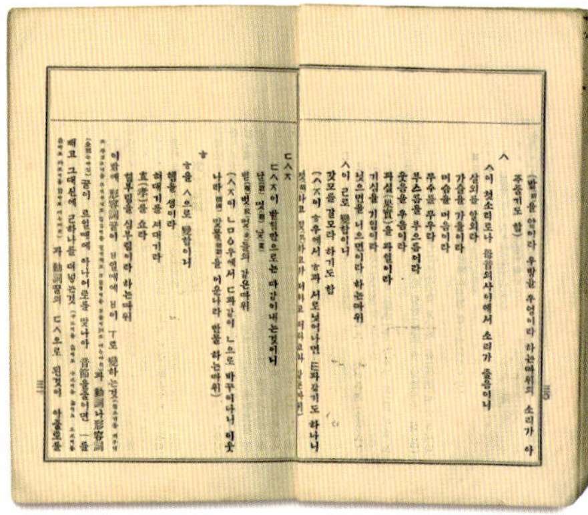

Joseon eomun gyeongwi, a Korean language study book written by Gwon Deok-gyu, 1923, Bumwoosa Publishing Co.

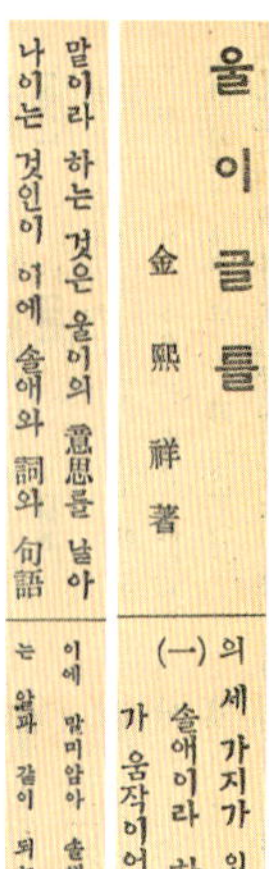

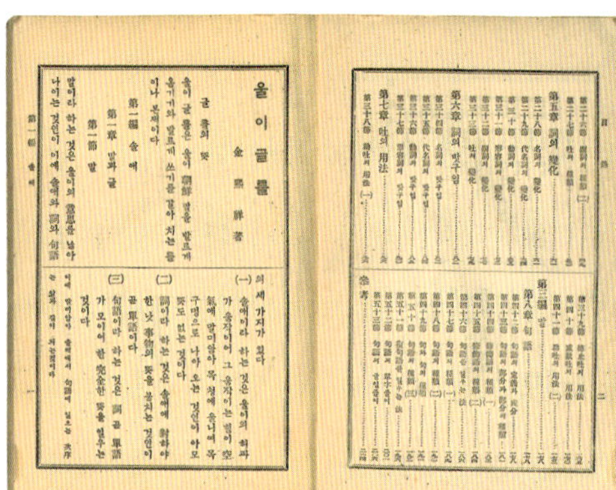

Uligeulteul, a Korean language grammar book written by Kim Hui-sang, 1927, Printed with metal type, Bumwoosa Publishing Co.

Establishment of the "Proposal for Unified Korean Orthography"

The "Proposal for Unified Korean Orthography" is a draft for unified Korean spelling rules enacted and promulgated by the Korean Language Society (currently the Korean Language Academy) in 1933 after collecting various scholars' opinions on the spelling rules widely used at the time. The proposal, which systemized Korean spelling principles, consisted of 65 clauses including generalities, particulars, and appendices. According to the decision at the annual meeting of the then Korean Language Society held on December 13, 1930, committee members were appointed to draft a unified Korean spelling system; the draft was thoroughly reviewed and revised several times and finally made public in commemoration of the 487th anniversary of the proclamation of Hangeul in 1933.

The final document was composed of three parts: introduction, generalities, and particulars. The first chapter of the particulars deals with the number and names of consonants and vowels of Hangeul; the second chapter with issues related to sounds such as tense sounds, palatalization, and the sound of final consonant ㄷ; the third chapter with Korean language grammar including notation of substantives and particles, stems and endings, regular predicates and irregular predicates, and final consonants, etymology of words, compounding of word classes, and prefixes; the fourth chapter separately deals with Chinese characters, along with acronyms, loanword orthography, and spacing.

The introductory part describes the preparation process for the "Proposal for Unified Korean Orthography" led by the Korean Language Society. The project was inagurated in 1930 and the first draft was produced by twelve committee members: Gwon Deok-gyu, Kim Yun-gyeong, Park Hyeon-sik, Sin Myeong-gyun, Lee Geuk-ro, Lee Byeong-gi, Lee Yun-jae, Lee Hui-seung, Jang Ji-yeong,

Jeong Yeol-mo, Jeong In-seop, and Choe Hyeon-bae. Additional committee members were appointed, bringing the number to eighteen. They included Kim Seon-gi, Lee Gap, Lee Man-gyu, Lee Sang-chun, Lee Se-jeong, and Lee Tak. All eighteen members undertook revision of the original draft. A separate ten-member committee (Gwon Deok-gyu, Kim Seon-gi, Kim Yun-gyeong, Sin Myeong-gyun, Lee Geuk-ro, Lee Yun-jae, Lee Hui-seung, Jang Ji-yeong, Jeong In-seop, and Choe Hyeon-bae) carried out the second round of revision. After a few rounds of revision, the finalized draft proposal was passed at the general meeting of the Korean Language Society on October 19, 1933.

The introductory part of the proposal gave an account of the three-year preparation process, noting that to produce the proposal for a unified Korean spelling system scores of people were enlisted over three years and 125 meetings were held during the period.

The following is an excerpt from the presentation paper.

> The Korean Language Society has established the "Proposal for Unified Korean Orthography" for promulgation to the public.
>
> The preparation process for the proposal is briefly explained as follows: At the general meeting of the Korean Language Society held on December 13, 1930 it was decided to establish a proposal for a unified Korean spelling system and 12 scholars were initially appointed to the committee. The 12 memebrs are Gwon Deok-gyu, Kim Yun-gyeong, Park Hyeon-sik, Sin Myeong-gyun, Lee Geuk-ro, Lee Byeong-gi, Lee Yun-jae, Lee Hui-seung, Jang Ji-yeong, Jeong Yeol-mo, Jeong In-seop, and Choe Hyeon-bae. The committee finally completed the draft proposal in December 1932, almost two years after the committee's formation. And then, another six members were added to the committee, which increased the number of members to 18. The newly appointed

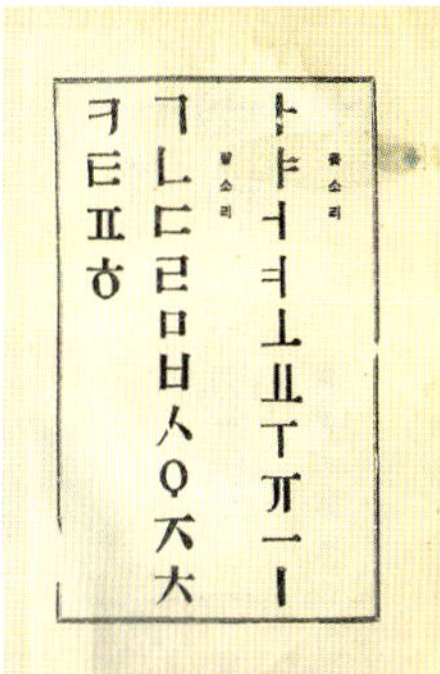

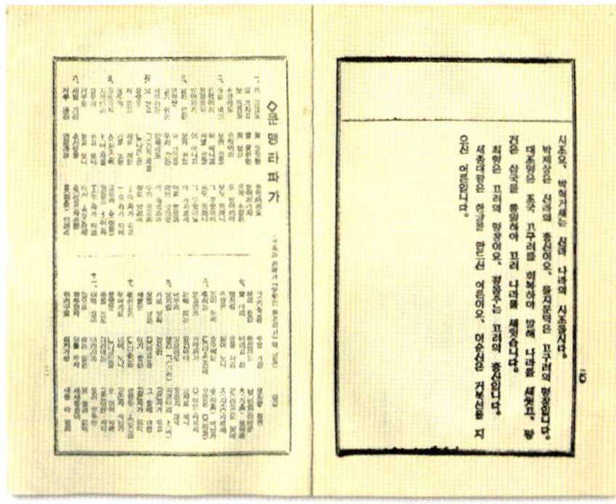

A Study of Hangeul written by Lee Yun-jae,
1933, Printed with metal type, Bumwoosa Publishing Co.

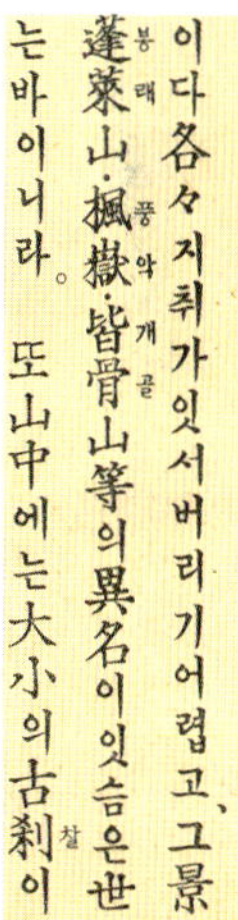

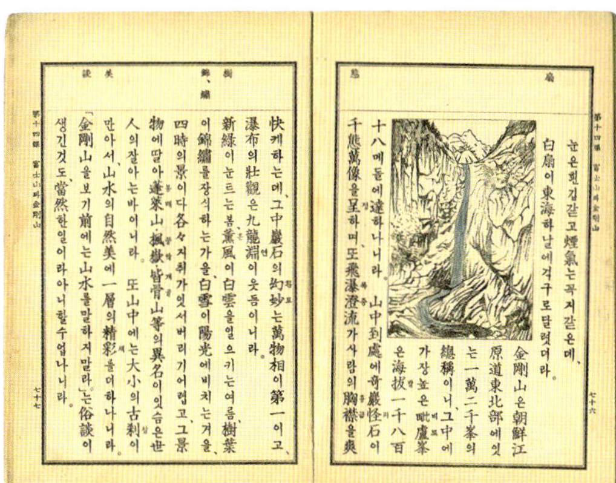

***Basic Reader of the Korean Language*,**
Volume 6, 1935, Printed with metal type, Samseong Museum of Publishing

members were Kim Seon-gi, Lee Gap, Lee Man-gyu, Lee Sang-chun, Lee Se-jeong, and Lee Tak. The 18-member committee held the first reading between December 25, 1932 and January 4, 1933 in Gaeseong, North Korea in order to discuss the proposal article by article. After the meeting, a ten-member committee was reorganized to make a revision of the draft. The ten members were Gwon Deok-gyu, Kim Seon-gi, Kim Yun-gyeong, Sin Myeong-gyun, Lee Geuk-ro, Lee Yun-jae, Lee Hui-seung, Jang Ji-yeong, Jeong In-seop, and Choe Hyeon-bae. Six months later, the revision process almost came to an end, and the second reading was held at Hawgyesa Temple with all 18 members participating in order to review the revised draft. The second reading lasted from July 25 to August 3, 1933. Right after the reading, a nine-member committee was again formed to finalize the draft to reflect recommendations made in the reading. The nine members were Gwon Deok-gyu, Kim Seon-gi, Kim Yun-gyeong, Sin Myeong-gyun, Lee Geuk-ro, Lee Yun-jae, Lee Hui-seung, Jeong In-seop, and Choe Hyeon-bae. The final draft produced by the nine-member committee was passed at a provisional general meeting of the Korean Language Society on October 19, enabling the proposed unified Korean spelling system to be enforced. Hence the "Proposal for Unified Korean Orthography" has now been completed.

As outlined above, it took three years for the proposal for the unified spelling system to be completed. The preparation involved 125 meetings, equivalent to 433 hours. The long painstaking process shows that organizing a spelling system is not an easy task. The Korean Language Society and those involved in the preparation process put all their effort into the project, considering all things strictly and most carefully, to produce the proposal for unified rules on spelling. Hence, we now officially announce the proposal to the public. However, this is just our first step toward systemizing Korean spelling principles, which are currently very confusing. Accordingly, it would not be right for us to claim that the proposal is without drawbacks. Besides, with the march of the times changes have subsequently taken place in various academic fields and Hangeul is no exception. So the Korean Language Society continues to keep its eyes on current developments in the public usage of Hangeul and looks forward to suggestions for improvement of Korean spelling rules.

Finally, we would like to express our sincere gratitude to all of those who have given their help and support for the establishment of the proposal. In particular, we want to extend our heartfelt thanks to Gong Tak, Song Jin-u, Kim Seong-su, and Hanseong Publishing Company.

On the 487th anniversary of the Promulgation of Hangeul
The Korean Language Society

The Generalities of the "Proposal for Unified Korean Orthography" are as follows:

Generalities

1. The unified spelling system makes it a rule to write down standard speech as it sounds, according to the rules of speech.
2. Standard speech refers to the language currently widely used among the middle-class residents of Seoul.
3. A space is placed between each word, but particles must be attached to the word in front without spacing.

According to the generalities above, the unified spelling principles define that the rules are to be applied to the standard language, that correspondence should be achieved between sounds and letters, and that in the case of the origin of the word being revealed and the word being written as it sounds, the word needs to be written according to the rules of speech.[24] Standard speech is confined to the speech that, in principle, is used by the middle-class in Seoul, but exceptions are possible. In addition, the rules also state that spacing must be applied to each word and particles be regarded as an independent part of speech but must be attached to the word in front.

24. When it comes to the representation of sounds and letters, it can be explained only with synchronic rules, then underlying forms need to be given. On the other hand, if it cannot be explained only with synchronic rules because it follows past historical rules, then it needs to be written as it sounds.

3. Fall of the Nation and Crisis of Hangeul

Japan, having forcibly annexed Korea in 1910, alternately used policies of appeasement and coercion in a bid to take control of Joseon until its collapse in 1945. In the later part of its occupation, however, Japan implemented a policy of Korean language annihilation, the likes of which is unprecedented in the history of humanity. Japan increased oppression of the Korean people after the Manchurian Incident of 1931 and promulgated the "Probation Decree on Korean Thought Criminals" in 1936, cracking down on Korean intellectuals who resisted Japan's colonial rule and keeping watch on Korean political offenders.

From the 1940s when Japan waged a war of aggression against foreign countries, the country adopted a policy for deliberate annihilation of Korea's racial and cultural identity. As parts of such efforts, Japan carried out a colonial policy aimed at transforming Koreans into Japanese imperial subjects. In order to obliterate Koreans' ethnic identity, it forced Koreans to change their names to Japanese names and denied them use of the Korean language. That is, Japan drove Korean language education out of public schools and offered students courses in Japanese only, forcing them to use Japanese at school.

Imperial Seal of the Daehan Empire, 19th century, National Museum of Korea

Government-General of Korea

The Government-General of Korea was an administrative body created by Japan to overthrow the Daehan Empire and rule Korea. It existed from the signing of the Korea-Japan Annexation Treaty on October 1, 1910 until September 2, 1945, when the US and Russia began to station troops on the Korean Peninsula.

The Japanese Government-General was created to succeed the Office of the Resident-General that had been established in 1905. From the first governor-general, Terauchi Masatake, to the ninth, Abe Nobuyuki, this powerful position was filled by an army or navy general. On March 1, 1914 an administrative reshuffle in local governments was carried out in accordance with Ordinance No. 111 of the Government-General (issued on December 29, 1913), and colonial rule over the Korean people began in earnest. The Japanese officially ruled over the Korean Peninsula for five days after their defeat in World War II and remained in place until it turned sovereignty over the south of the 38th parallel to the US military government on September 3, 1945.

Nation obliteration policy

While Japan alternately used policies of appeasement and coercion as mentioned above, in principle it stubbornly maintained a policy of deliberate annihilation of Korea's racial and cultural identity. The obliteration policy started formally with the Educational Ordinance for Korea. The first Educational Ordinance, issued in August 1911, was designed to strengthen colonial education for Koreans, and the second Educational Ordinance, a revision made after the March First Independence Movement of 1919, was issued by the then Governor-

General Saito as an appeasement strategy under the name of "cultural politics." Then the third Educational Ordinance for Korea was announced in 1938 to reinforce the policy of transforming Koreans into subjects of the Japanese Empire. Under the third ordinance, Japanese history and the Japanese language became mandatory subjects while the Korean language was degraded to an elective. The fourth Educational Ordinance issued in March 1943 placed emphasis on educating Koreans in accordance with the ways of the Japanese Empire and students and schools began to be exploited as a base for war preparation.

In order to strengthen its colonial policies of imbuing Koreans with the idea that Japan and Joseon are one and of transforming them into subjects of the Japanese Empire, the Japanese Government-General forced the use of the Japanese language (and conversely obliterate Korean) while attempting to find theoretical justification for the claim that the two languages belong to the same language family. To encourage the spread of Japanese, in February 1937 director of the Domestic Affairs Bureau Odake issued a ban on the use of Korean interpreters in all government agencies, thus enforcing the exclusive use of Japanese.

Besides the ban on the use of Korean, in July 1938 the Japanese Government-General tightened control over the publication of Korean books as a pretext for saving paper, and consolidated or discontinued publications written in Korean including bulletins, brochures, and official magazines. As a result, two daily newspapers, the *Dong-A Ilbo* and the *Chosun Ilbo* were forced to cease publication in August 1940. This was followed by the closure of 21 magazines, including the monthly magazine *Munjang* and the literary magazine *Sahaegongnon* by May 1941.

Following is a summary of the policies implemented by Japan in order to deliberately annihilate the Korean language and national identity.

1. Ban imposed on the teaching and use of Korean
2. Discontinuation of the publication of Korean newspapers and magazines including the *Chosun Ilbo* and *Dong-A Ilbo*
3. Oppression of Korean language scholars
4. Forcing Koreans to recite the "Oath of Imperial Subjects" and visit Shinto shrines
5. Forcing Koreans to adopt Japanese names
6. Promoting the idea that Korea and Japan are one and that the two countries have common ancestors.

Name change order

The name change order is a policy that was implemented by Japan between February 1940 and August 1945, right before liberation, which forced Koreans to adopt Japanese names.

On November 10, 1939, the Japanese Government-General amended the Korean Civil Ordinance that compelled Koreans to change their names to Japanese ones between February 11 and August 10, 1940. The gist of the revised ordinance was that within six months the head of every family should abandon his Korean name and adopt a Japanese one and register such name with the authorities.

Some pro-Japanese collaborators voluntarily changed their names as soon as the ordinance went into effect. However, as of May 1940, three months later, the number of households that had obeyed the order stood at a mere 7.6 percent of the total population. Hence, the Japanese Government-General adopted vicious and coercive measures to force Koreans to change their names, and raised the rate to 79.3 percent. These coercive measures are outlined as follows:

1. Children from families maintaining Korean surnames will not be admitted by any educational institution in Korea.
2. Teachers are to scold and give corporal punishment to children with Korean names for no reason, motivating children to pester their parents to adopt a Japanese family name.
3. Those maintaining Korean names should not be employed by any public and private organization and any employees with Korean names should to be gradually laid off.
4. Administrative organizations should not handle any civil complaints filed by Koreans who do not have Japanese surnames.
5. The police should put the name of those who still use Korean surnames on the blacklist of independent activists and unpatriotic citizens and carry out thorough inspections on them.
6. Koreans who resist changing their names must be the first drafted for compulsory labor.
7. Koreans who do not change their names will not be supplied with rations and commodities.
8. Railway freight with Korean name tags will not be transported.

In Korea, one's surname indicates membership of a certain family clan, and one of the two syllables of the given name indicates one's rank within the family. The name hence reveals the genealogy and identity of an individual. By forcing Koreans to change such names into Japanese names, Japan attempted to obliterate Koreans' traditional way of thinking. The fall of Japan in August 1945 in the Pacific War freed Koreans from the name change order. In 1946, the U.S. and Russian military governments that were stationed on the Korean

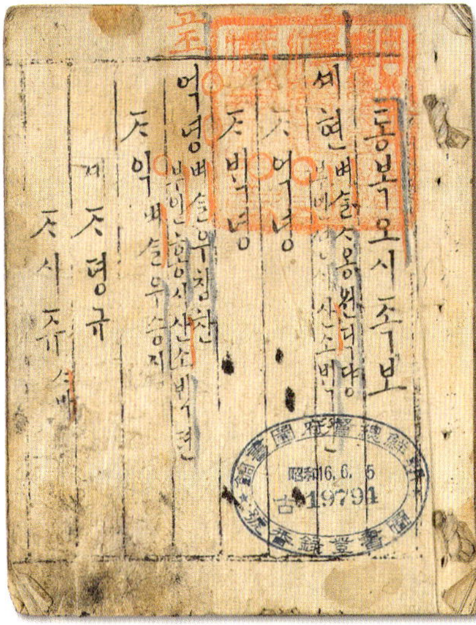

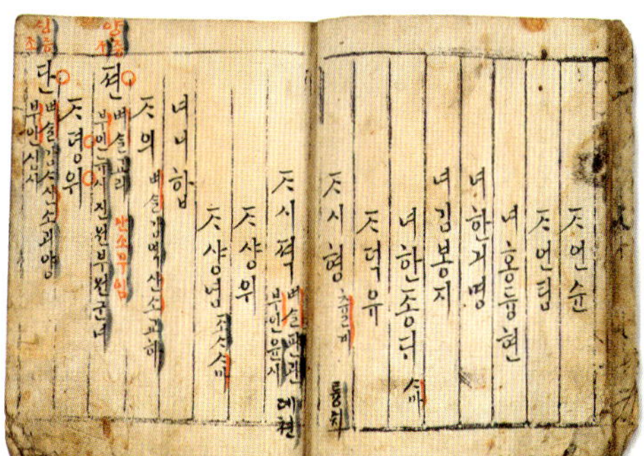

Genealogical record book of the Oh clan from Dongbok

Peninsula instituted a measure that enabled Koreans to regain their original names.

The Korean Language Society Incident

The most effective way to annihilate a nation is to eliminate its language and writing system. With the issuance of the Ordinance on Korean Language Education, Japan attempted to decrease or to limit teaching of the Korean language while expanding the ban on the use of the Korean language. In addition, persecution of Hangeul scholars intensified.

Research on Hangeul led by Ju Si-gyeong flourished around 1900 when Japan's invasion of Joseon intensified. When Korea came under Japanese colonial rule in 1910, research efforts were stepped up as a way of protecting the national spirit. In December 1921, the Korean Language Research Society was founded and Hangeul scholars were encouraged to continue research. In October 1929, a Korean dictionary compilation committee was formed. The committee conducted research on and organized general rules of the Korean language as a preliminary study for dictionary compilation. Research outcomes include the "Proposal for Unified Korean Orthography," "Inspection of the Standard Language," and "Loanword Orthography," which were immediately translated into educational movements dedicated to preserving Korean language.

As aforementioned, Hangeul research during the Japanese occupation period was in line with movements to protect the spirit and the native language of the nation. Hence, toward the end of the period Japan adopted oppressive policies that cracked down on Hangeul research and banned the use of the Korean language. In 1936, Japan promulgated the Probation Decree on Korean Thought Criminals, which led to the arrest of members of the Cultivation Friendship Association, an enlightenment organization, in 1937, and of members of the Heungeop Club, an anti-Japanese movement organization, in 1938. In 1941, Japan announced the Prevention Custody Decree on Korean Thought Criminals that enabled it to arbitrarily imprison those involved in Korean nationalist movements and enlightenment activities.

In October 1942, the Korean Language Society Incident took place. Members of the society and related figures, who were actively involved in activities to defend the spoken and written Korean language to fight against Japan's nation obliteration policy, were arrested and put on trial. The following excerpt from the *Encyclopedia of Korean Culture* describes the case.

> Against this historical background, Park Yeong-ok, a student of Yeongsaeng Girls' High School in Hamheung, North Korea, was caught on the train conversing with her friends in Korean and interrogated by a Korean police officer named Yasda.
>
> During the interrogation of the school girls, the police found that the person who had imbued those girls with nationalistic spirit was Jeong Tae-jin, who had participated in the compilation of a Korean-language dictionary in Seoul. On September 5 the same year, Jeong Tae-jin was taken to the police and investigated. During his interrogation, the police squeezed out a confession that the Korean Language Society is a nationalist group dedicated to the independence movement.
>
> Using this incident as an excuse, Japan banned the movement to spread Hangeul, which had been revived after the March First Independence Movement, dissolved organizations that impeded the policy of the enslavement of Koreans, and rounded up the leading Korean intellectuals.

On October 1 the same year, 11 Hangeul scholars including Lee Jung-hwa, Jang Ji-yeong, and Choe Hyeon-bae were arrested in Seoul and the following day were sent to Hongwon in Hamgyeongnam-do Province. Those involved in the Korean Language Society were soon apprehended one after another, and as of April 1, 1943 a total of 33 people were under custody. As many as 48 Korean witnesses were put through tortuous interrogations.

The Hongwon Police Station, where the interrogations were conducted, charged 33 Koreans who were directly involved in the dictionary compilation, had provided financial assistance, or were supportive of the Hangeul research institute with violation of the Security Maintenance Law.

The police station submitted to the prosecution a written opinion as follows: 24 people should be prosecuted, including Lee Geuk-ro, Lee Yun-jae, Choe Hyeon-bae, Lee Hui-seung, Jeong In-seung, Kim Yun-gyeong, Kim Yang-su, Kim Do-yeon, Lee U-sik, Lee Jung-wha, Kim Beop-rin, Lee In, Han Jing, Jeong Yeol-mo, Jang Ji-yeong, Jang Hyeon-sik, Lee Man-gyu, Lee Gang-rae, Kim Seon-gi, Jeong In-seop, Lee Byeong-gi, Lee Eun-sang, Seo Min-ho, and Jeong Tae-jin; another 6 should be suspended of indictment, including Sin Yun-guk, Kim Jong-cheol, Lee Seok-rin, Gwon Seung-uk, Seo Seung-hyo, Yun Byeong-ho; An Jae-hong should not be indicted; Gwon Deok-gyu and An Ho-sang should be granted a stay of prosecution.

The prosecution indicted 16 people, including Lee Geuk-ro, Lee Yun-jae, Choe Hyeon-bae, Lee Hui-seung, Jeong In-seung, Jeong Tae-jin, Kim Yang-su, Kim Do-yeon, Lee U-sik, Lee Jung-wha, Kim Beop-rin, Lee In, Han Jing, Jeong Yeol-mo, Jang Ji-yeong, Jang Hyeon-sik; 12 people were suspended of indictment. Those who were indicted were brought to preliminary trial and the rest were discharged. Those indicted were detained at Hamheung Prison. On December 8 the same year,

Lee Yun-jae died in jail and Han Jing also died in jail on February 22, 1944; Jang Ji-yeong and Jeong Yeol-mo were released from prison due to expiration of the statute of limitations; as a result, a total of 12 were brought to trial.

According to the written judgment of the preliminary trial issued by the Hamheung provincial court of justice that read, "Given that the native language serves as a means of cultivating national consciousness, the dictionary compilation led by the Korean Language Society can be viewed as a form of nationalist movement to preserve the national spirit of Korea," the 12 Koreans were charged with rebellion. The trials, which lasted from December 1944 to January 1945, were held nine times in the Hamheung provincial court. Lee Geuk-ro was sentenced to six years in jail, Choe Hyeon-bae to four years, Lee Hui-seung to two and a half years, and Jeong In-seung and Jeong Tae-jin to two years each. Kim Beop-rin, Lee Jung-wha, Lee U-sik, Kim Yang-su, Kim Do-yeon, Lee In were sentenced to two years in jail with a stay of execution of three years; Jang Hyeon-sik was free of charges.

Accordingly, those who received a stay of execution and were found not guilty were acquitted. Among those who were sentenced to imprisonment, Jeong Tae-jin gave up appeal to a higher court believing that completing his sentence would be faster than filing an appeal. He was freed from prison on July 1, 1945 after serving his time. Lee Geuk-ro, Choe Hyeon-bae, Lee Hui-seung, and Jeong In-seung filed appeals, but the appeals were dismissed on August 13. But Korea was liberated two days later, so they were freed from prison on August 17, 1945.

V. Hangeul in the World

After liberation from Japanese colonial rule, Korea saw unprecedentedly rapid economic development in a short period of time. Rising up from the ashes of internecine war, which had broken out right after liberation, the country made remarkable economic achievements. Currently, Korea is one of the world's biggest economies and is in a position enviable enough for the term "Korean dream" to be coined.

As Korean pop culture spreads rapidly around the world, a phenomenon known as Hallyu, the number of foreigners seeking to learn Korean is growing just as fast. It seems that globalization of the Korean language and Hangeul is just around the corner. Korea's remarkable strides on the economic and cultural fronts can largely be attributed to the existence of Hangeul, one of the world's most scientific and systematic writhing systems. In commemoration of Hangeul, the National Hangeul Museum has recently been opened.

1. Birth of a New Korea
2. Hangeul Museums
3. Why the World Admires Hangeul

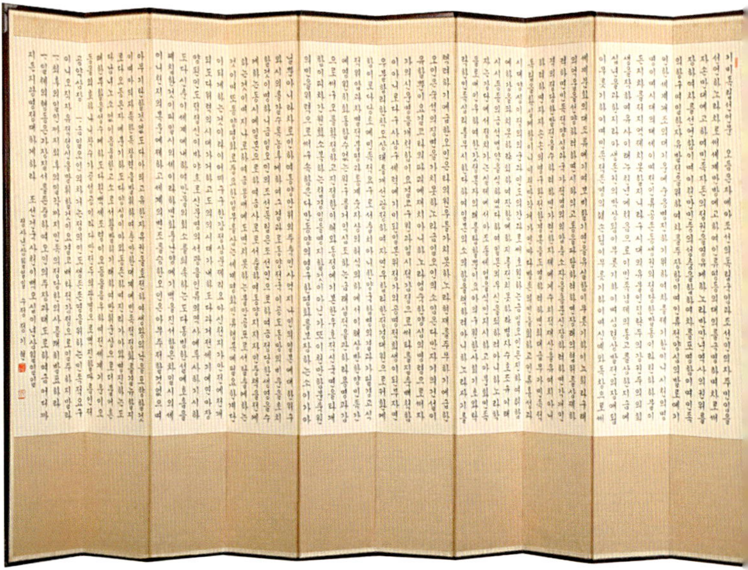

Folding Screen of the 1919 Declaration of Independence in Hangeul,
Sogang University Museum

1. Birth of a New Korea

The end of the Second World War in 1945 coincided with Korea's independence from Japanese colonial rule. Three years later, when the Korean peninsula had been divided into South and North, a new government was established in the South. But in 1950, war broke out between the South and North and lasted for almost three years. At the time, Korea was one of the poorest countries in the world. But since the 1960s, Korea has succeeded in industrialization and democratization and continued its unprecedented rapid economic growth.

Korea's GDP, which stood at a mere 4.24 trillion won (Bank of Korea statistics) in 1972, exceeded 56 trillion won in 1982, a more than 13-fold increase in 10 years. Forty years later, the GDP figure skyrocketed to 1,237 trillion won, nearly a 300 times increase.

Korea's national income has also jumped exponentially. In the 1970s, the gross national income increased by eleven times over the previous decade, by four times in the 1980s, by about three times in the 1990s, and by two times in the 2000s. That is, Korea's GNI grew by almost 400 times over the past 40 years.

As Korea lacks resources, its economic growth depends heavily on international trade. In the three decades between 1980 and 2009, the country's exports increased by 22 times, while its imports rose by 14 times. Accordingly, the trade balance, which had previously suffered a chronic deficit, shifted to a surplus in 1986. The surplus was maintained until the end of the 1980s before trade edged back into the red from the early to mid-1990s. From 1998 to the present trade has continued to mark a surplus.

From 2011, Korea surpassed the one trillion-dollar mark in trade for the second consecutive year and recorded a trade surplus of 28.6 billion dollars in 2012. As a result, Korea's foreign reserve holdings, which stood at 580 million dollars in 1970, jumped to over 300 billion dollars as of 2012. This figure indicates more than 1,000 times growth over some 40 years. Korea ranked 13th in global trade in 2002 and continued to show remarkable growth to become the world's 8th largest trader a decade later.

*Korea's rank in international trade

13th in 2002, 12th in 2003, 11th in 2007, 10th in 2009, 9th in 2010, and 8th in 2012

External forces of globalization

Worldwide spread of overseas Koreans

With improved international recognition of Korea, the number of Koreans emigrating from the country has decreased but the number of Koreans of either Korean or foreign nationality residing abroad has continued to increase. The number of overseas Koreans stood at around 6.8 million in 2009 and rose to approximately 7.2 million in 2011. As Koreans reside in Africa and Europe as well as China, Japan and the U.S., once considered the land of dreams, it can be said there is no country where Koreans cannot be found. Koreans are indeed scattered all over the world: in the case of Kiribati in Asia, there is only one Korean national, but in China there are as many

as 2.7 million.
These overseas Koreans are helping each other, leading various forms of community life by forming various organizations such as Korean community associations, Korean businessmen associations, and Korean overseas student associations. (According to data from the Ministry of Foreign Affairs and Trade, there are 2,989 organizations of overseas Korean nationals.) In Africa, there are 57 Korean organizations, 5 of which are found in Tanzania.

The largest populations of overseas Koreans can be found in China and Japan. Japan has more Koreans with permanent resident status, whereas China has more Koreans with citizenship. A total of 461,127 Koreans are residing in 32 countries in the rest of Asia and Oceania, from as few as a single resident to as many as 100,000 in a certain country. In Europe, 656,707 overseas Koreans are living in 52 countries; in the Middle East region, 16,302 in 19 countries; and in Africa, 11,072 in 42 countries.

Spread of Korean language education overseas

In the U.S., Korean language classes are held in 1,000 places on weekends, mostly led by overseas Koreans. In addition, dozens of American secondary schools include Korean in their curricula, while countless universities offer Korean language courses. With the rising popularity of the Korean language, it has been adopted as an elective in the American university entrance examination, and the Foundation for Korean Language and Culture in the U.S. is now striving to spread high-level Korean language in American high schools by introducing credit transfer programs between high schools and universities.

The popularity of the Korean language has been explosive in China and Japan. In China, the number of universities offering

Korean language courses (no distinction made with "Joseon language") before the establishment of diplomatic ties between China and South Korea was only five: Peking University, University of International Business and Economics, Luoyang Foreign Language University, Beijing International Studies University, and Yanbian University. As of 2011, however, the number exceeded 200. Related academic societies composed of more than 200 professors hold conferences every year. Such conditions suggest that in China the Korean language is now viewed as a field worthy of research rather than something to learn out of interest. In Japan (subtle distinction made between Korean language and "Joseon language"), the number of people who want to learn Korean is steadily increasing, as indicated by the high sales of textbooks for a Korean language educational program broadcast on NHK.

The number of people learning Korean has also shown explosive growth in the Southeast Asian region. The Philippines, Indonesia, Thailand, Malaysia, and Vietnam are now offering Korean language courses and Korean language schools are available for the children of immigrants. If such growing worldwide popularity continues, the Korean language may obtain the status of an international language someday in the future.

The International Korean Language Foundation and the King Sejong Institute

From the late 20th century, the number of foreign learners of the Korean language overseas and in Korea has jumped. To respond effectively to this surge in popularity, the International Korean Language Foundation was established as a private foundation under the jurisdiction of the Ministry of Culture, Sports and Tourism on January 13, 2001. The foundation was mainly engaged in projects related to the promotion and dissemination of the Korean language at home and abroad; projects related to Korean language education for foreigners; survey and research on promotion of the Korean language; and carrying out entrusted projects for the promotion of the Korean language.

The private International Korean Language Foundation had carried out projects related to the globalization of Korean for almost a decade before handing over such business to the state-funded King Sejong Institute Foundation in 2012. The latter foundation is a legal entity established to undertake businesses related to operation of the King Sejong Institute, an educational institute devoted to propagation of the Korean language and culture to learners of Korean as a foreign or second language.

Management of the King Sejong Institute was initially the responsi-

Staff and students of the King Sejong Institute, the Philippines, on a retreat bility of the National Institute of the Korean Language but is now under the Ministry of Culture, Sports and Tourism. As of 2015, 139 branches of the King Sejong Institute are in operation in 54 countries with the aim of providing more opportunities to foreigners who want to learn Hangeul, the Korean language, and Korean culture.

The goals of the King Sejong Institute are as follows:

1. To activate cultural exchange on the principle of interculturalism
2. To provide foreigners or Koreans overseas with opportunities to learn the Korean language
3. To develop a leading brand of Korean language education

To achieve these goals, the following projects are carried out:

- Designation and support of organizations or lecture programs that teach Korean as a foreign or second language and promote Korean culture as King Sejong Institutes
- Development and operation of online educators in Korean as a foreign or second language and Korean culture as Nuri-King Sejong Institutes
- Distribution of standardized Korean language curriculum and textbooks
- Training of Korean language teachers and support for dispatch of teachers to King Sejong Institutes
- Education in Korean culture and publicity
- Other projects as required to spread Korean as a second or foreign language

Internal globalization: Formation of a Korean-style multicultural society

The history of humankind has been marked by the recurrence of war and peace and the struggle between the dominant and the subordinate; cultures repeatedly clash with each other and new cultures emerge dominant, which rise and then fall over time. Repetition of this whole process is what history is all about. In such a struggle, when more than two cultures coexist and create a multicultural society, such a society generally takes one of three forms.

1. American style: Many different peoples move to a new world and create a society where the initially dominant race coexists with the races that come afterwards.
2. Chinese style: With territorial expansion, the dominant race coexists with the minority peripheral races.
3. European style: Laborers of different races move to a technologically advanced society forming a society where the existing order and the immigrant order coexist.

Since the end of the 20th century, however, a new style of multicultural society has been taking shape in Korea and Japan.

4. Korean style: This is a complex multicultural society where immigrant workers, immigrant workers who have married Koreans, and the children of intercultural marriages are intertwined.

Demographic composition of immigrants

As of 2011, when Korea's population exceeded the 50 million

mark, the share of foreigners residing in Korea reached 2.5 percent. Among them 111,110 foreigners were naturalized Korean citizens.

Increase and decrease in international marriages

The number of Koreans marrying foreign partners surged from the late 1990s. However, the upward trend began to retreat from 2005 when the percentage of international marriages among the total reached a peak of 13.5 percent. As of 2011, international marriages made up nine percent of the total marriages. In most cases, such marriages comprised a female foreigner marrying a Korean man.

Nationality of foreigners

Foreign women who married Korean men mostly came from China, however their share in total international marriages has continued to fall over the years and in 2011 they were finally overtaken by Vietnamese women. The combined share of Chinese and Vietnamese women amounted to 68.2 percent of foreign women marrying Korean men. Meanwhile, men of Chinese, Japanese, and American nationalities were found to account for a combined share of 69.5 percent of foreign men marrying Korean women.

Development of Korean language policy

As the era of English as the universal language of the world began with the turn of the 21st century, languages other than English and a few that are used by populous races face an existential threat. Against this historical condition, the Korean language today faces some special challenges.

First, the Korean language is losing ground even in everyday life as well as academic use as the importance of English grows in the country.

Second, in line with Korea's remarkable economic progress, there has been unprecedented growth in the number of Korean language learners in China, Japan, and Southeast Asia.

Third, a unique form of multicultural society is taking shape in Korea.

Fourth, the existence of the humanities, including language, in the purely academic sense, is being endangered by industrialization and commercialization.

In response to such circumstances, the National Institute of the Korean Language is now making provisions for policy development as follows:

> In order to develop language policies and create a favorable environment for policy implementation, the National Institute of the Korean Language is now pursuing various projects defined by the Framework Act on the Korean Language including development plans for the Korean language, and operation of the National Language Deliberation Council and Chief Korean Language Officer System. The institute is also carrying out exchange with international institutes related to language policies and the implementation of projects for inter-Korean language exchange.
>
> Based on the Framework Act on the Korean Language enacted in 2005, the basic plan for development of the Korean language was established in 2006. Under this plan, a report on measures implemented to improve and preserve the native language and the outcomes of the related measures are to be submitted every two years to the National Assembly.

In addition, the basic plan is to be amended every five years.

The Framework Act on the Korean Language stipulates that central and local government agencies appoint Chief Korean Language Officers responsible for tasks related to the development and preservation of the Korean language. In line with the provision, central and local government agencies have chief officers in place, and the National Institute of the Korean Language holds a conference on policies for improvement of Korean language ability and a meeting of the Korean language officials every year in order to create a favorable environment where central and local government agencies can implement various policies for development of the Korean language. In addition, the process of making provisions for amendment of the Framework Act on the Korean Language is now underway based on problems that emerged during the actual implementation of the policies. Three subcommittee meetings were held in 2007 as part of the amendment process. As of now, a Chief Korean Language Officer is present in 459 central and local government agencies, including 54 central administrative agencies, 163 organizations affiliated with the central agencies, and 16 metropolitan municipalities, and 226 local government agencies.

The National Institute of the Korean Language continues to follow up policy trends in international language institutions and carry out exchange projects with language policy-making institutions in major countries. It has conducted a survey on international language policy institutions and has made continuous efforts to increase mutual understanding with the National Institute for Japanese Language and Linguistics including the invitation of each other's researchers from 2004.

Furthermore, in preparation for future unification of the two Koreas, the National Institute of the Korean Language has continued to pursue language exchange projects with North Korea. It is also planning to hold an annual conference of linguists from the two Koreas and seeking various projects with the aim of recovering linguistic homogeneity between North and South Korea. (Excerpted from the introduction to the projects of the National Institute of the Korean Language, 2007)

Digital Hangeul Museum

2. Hangeul Museums

The Digital Hangeul Museum

The Digital Hangeul Museum (http://www.hangeulmuseum.org) first began as a project led by the International Korean Language Foundation (predecessor to the King Sejong Institute Foundation) in 2001, prior to foundation of the National Hangeul Museum, for the collection of materials to promote Hangeul around the world. In 2002, the digital museum opened two sections on the history and artistry of Hangeul. As of 2013 the cyber museum has a total of eight sections: "Birth and History of Hangeul," "Beautiful Hangeul," "Hangeul in Everyday Life," "Hangeul and Education," "Evolution of Hangeul and Its Future," "Special Exhibitions," "Hangeul Games" and "Academic Information Hall."

The "Birth and History of Hangeul" section offers information on not only the invention and development of Hangeul and the history of Koreans' literacy, but the history of the world's writing systems. The "Beautiful Hangeul" section provides information on the formative characteristics and fonts of Hangeul and gives examples. It also offers information related to Hangeul typography, art and the writing systems of the world, as well as the pictures made of Hangeul letters. The "Hangeul in Everyday Life" section shows the use of

Hangeul in the lives of the Korean people, particularly in relation to food, shelter, and clothing. The "Hangeul and Education" section offers information relevant to enhancing understanding of Hangeul and movements dedicated to its development, changes in Korean language textbooks and Korean language curricula, and teaching materials. In addition, regulations on Korean language and speech are also given including Korean orthography rules, standard language regulations, loanword orthography rules, and Romanization principles. The "Evolution of Hangeul and Its Future" section deals with issues related to the mechanization, informatization, and globalization of Hangeul. It also gives information on North Korea's informatization and norms, and on North's language purification campaigns. The "Special Exhibitions" section offers information related to special exhibitions since 2006. The "Hangeul Games" section provides six types of games including "Hangeul Guards" and "Hangeul Quiz."

Among the eight sections, "Academic Information Hall" can be said to contain the most salient information. The subsections include: literature and commentaries, the list of Hangeul-related materials, integrated information on materials written in Hangeul, and Chinese characters in ancient literature. The images of ancient literature written in Hangeul are given along with explanations. In particular, different commentaries are offered for specialists and for the general public. Accordingly, visitors to the cyber museum can use information on Hangeul literature according to their needs along with photographs and other pictures.

The National Hangeul Museum

Foundation of the National Hangeul Museum can be seen as the

National Hangeul Museum

outcome of Korea's remarkable economic growth, which has enabled the country to rank among the world's top traders, and the globalization of Hangeul in the late 20th and early 21st century. At the end of the 20th century when the creation of the Digital Hangeul Museum was on the drawing board, it was deemed practically impossible to secure the space and budget to build a real museum. Korea's international status and economic capability, however, have enabled creation of the National Hangeul Museum in the real world. The museum opened in October 2014, next door to the National Museum of Korea, located in Yongsan, Seoul.

The invention of Hangeul was an epoch-making event that opened a new chapter in the history of writing systems of humankind. As the Hunmin jeongeum, the original name of Hangeul, is a priceless human treasure it is important that the National Hangeul Museum be maintained as the world's largest and best museum dedicated to writing systems.

To become the world's largest such museum, it is necessary to collect as much data relevant to Hangeul as possible, and based on this information compile all materials related to writing systems in the history of mankind and secure sufficient space to display them. Priority, of course, must be placed on the collection and proper display of all data pertinent to letters and writing. For example, the traces of a pictograph found in Ulju County, Gyeongsangnam-do Province, should be restored to its original size and shape and be exhibited somewhere in the National Hangeul Museum. In addition, the various ancient letters that had existed around the world, and memorial steles and publications featuring those old writing systems should also be displayed at the museum. For example, in case of the steles and temples where ancient Egyptian hieroglyphics are engraved, 3D technology should be used to produce images that show their original form and size. Images of the epitaph of King Asoka of the Maurya Empire, a pertinent artifact in regard to unification of Indian script, and information on the dissemination of the Indian script should be available for viewing in the museum. In other words, all materials related to the writing systems of the world need to be accessible in some form in the National Hangeul Museum.

To become the best museum of its kind in the world, first, explanation and interpretation of every script that has ever existed in the history of human writing systems needs to be available at the National Hangeul Museum. Second, all facts pertinent to the shape and aesthetic function of written letters (characters) and their close relationship with the mental life of human beings need to be academically established, based on which the visual function of each letter should be reexamined in environmental and aesthetic terms. That such aspects of a writing system can contribute to the harmony and stability of human life needs to be validated and experimental structures supporting this argument should be available in the museum. Third, the National Hangeul Museum should also present a vision for the future by showing that the development of writing systems is related to the future of humanity, and that development of the industries concerned will determine the future of human beings. That is, the National Hangeul Museum should be able to present a balanced look at the past of humankind in relation to the development of writing systems, the present of humankind in relation to the function of writing systems, and the future of humankind in relation to technological advance.

Korea's remarkable economic progress is much indebted to Hangeul. Once one of the world's poorest countries, Korea has become an economically advanced one in a miraculously short time. In Korea's sudden rise, the information technology (IT) industry has played a crucial role, and no one would deny the fact that Hangeul has greatly contributed to its development. The advancement of Korea's computer and mobile technologies is directly related to the systematic structure and organization of Hangeul consonants and vowels, which enable people to use devices featuring the pertinent technologies with ease and convenience. All these benefits prove that Hangeul is a scientifically invented writing system.

Hangeul's scientific excellence and systematic structure will likely have a long-lasting effect on the future development of Korea and its IT industry. In this sense, the National Hangeul Museum needs to serve as a forum for display of the future direction of Korea's IT industry and the country's continuous efforts to pursue new possibilities.

3. Why the World Admires Hangeul

As of the 21st century, a numerous number of scripts are in use all over the world. Among them, the most widely used are the Roman alphabet and the Cyrillic alphabet. India, the Arab world, and Southeast Asian countries all have their own writing systems to use. However, UNESCO, in recognition of Hangeul's excellence, established the King Sejong Literacy Prize in 1989 to award those who contribute to the global effort to eradicate illiteracy. Moreover, the world renowned linguist J. McCawley has been commemorating Hangeul Day on October 9 every year for over twenty years.

Professor Geoffrey Sampson, an eminent specialist in writing systems, admired Hangeul, saying, "There is no doubt that Hangeul is the world's most scientifically excellent writing system." Indeed, Hangeul is widely recognized and admired by many of the world's renowned scholars. Why is that so?

Hangeul: The only alphabet whose creator and method of creation are known

Hangeul (originally called Humin jeongeum) was invented by King Sejong in January 1444. He then commissioned scholars including Jeong In-ji and Seong Sam-mun to produce a publication also titled *Hunmin jeongeum* that explained the reason and fundamental principles behind the creation of Hangeul in relation to Neo-Confucian principles. The *Hunmin jeongeum* was promulgated in September 1446.

King Sejong invented the Hunmin jeongeum by using all the knowledge he had about Neo-Confucianism and observing the sounds made by human beings and studying how they were made. Different peoples are able to learn foreign languages because all people make similar sounds and think in similar ways. In principle, people use their lips and tongues to make sounds. When they move their lower lip and tongue close to the upper lip, teeth, gums, front palate, and rear palate, sounds can be made. King Sejong understood these basic principles and reflected them in the creation of Hangeul.

Phonetic values of the letters reflected in their shapes

Due to the principles behind the design of the letters, it is possible to predict the relationship between the sound and the letter when it is seen. Among the initial consonants, the sound of ㅁ can be made when the lips are closed and then parted, the shape of the consonant being modeled after the shape of the mouth with the closed lips. The letter ㅂ was formed as a stronger sound than ㅁ but both are made by closing the lips. Likewise, the sound of the consonant ㅍ is much stronger than the sound of ㅂ and the letter was created by adding a stroke to the letter ㅂ. The consonant ㄴ was formed by tracing the shape of the tongue touching the upper gum section. To make a stronger sound, a stroke was added, which resulted in the letter ㄷ, and to make an even stronger sound another stroke was added to create the letter ㅌ. In the case of the letter ㄱ, it was formed in the shape of the rear part of the tongue touching the soft palate. Again, a

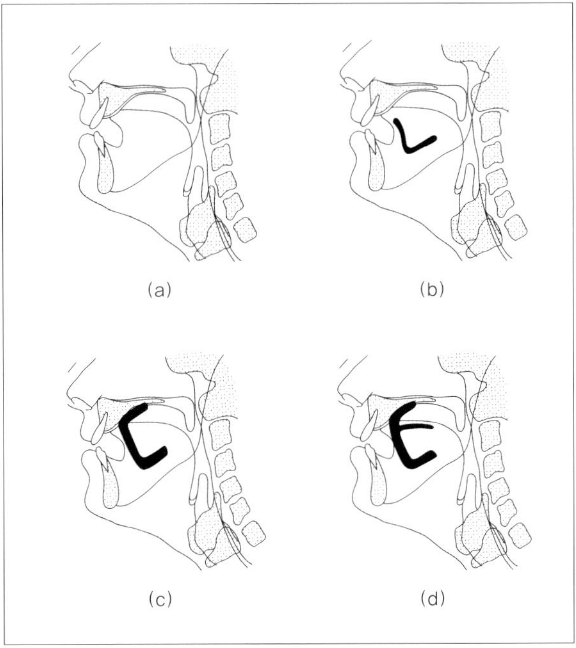

stroke was added to form ㅋ, which is a stronger sound than ㄱ. The letter ㅅ was formed by tracing the shape of the teeth. The shapes of the letters ㅈ and ㅊ are derived from the shape of the letter ㅅ by adding a stroke respectively according to the varying sounds. Lastly, the letter ㅇ was based on the circular shape of the throat; the shapes of letters ㆆ and ㅎ were derived from the shape of the letter ㅇ.

Due to these letter design principles, the sounds of letters with a common shape are articulated in the same location. And the letters with the more complicated forms have stronger sounds. The process of forming the letters ㄴ, ㄷ, ㅌ is seen in the picture on the facing page.

In principle, the shapes of Hangeul vowels were modeled after heaven (•), earth (ㅡ), and human beings (ㅣ). Based on these three letters, new letters were formed. Among these basic vowels, when the letter • in the shape of a dot is added to either the right side or left side of the vowel ㅣ in the shape of a vertical line, the resulting vowels are ㅏ and ㅓ, respectively. When the letter • is attached to either the top or bottom of the letter ㅡ in the shape of a horizontal line, the vowels ㅗ and ㅜ are formed, respectively. Again, when a separate stroke is added to the newly formed letters, the letters of ㅑ, ㅕ, ㅛ, ㅠ are formed. However, when a vertical line is added the vowels ㅐ, ㅔ, ㅚ, ㅟ are formed. Therefore, when these already formed letters are combined differently, the whole set of Hangeul vowels can be produced. The process of forming the shape of vowels is shown below.

Basic formation	•	ㅡ	ㅣ	
One dot plus one line	ㅏ	ㅓ	ㅗ	ㅜ
Two dots plus one line	ㅑ	ㅕ	ㅛ	ㅠ
One dot plus two lines	ㅐ	ㅔ	ㅚ	ㅟ

A new chapter in the world history of letters

The invention of Hangeul is of great importance in the history of human writing systems. First, its invention was of significance in that it gave the Korean people their own writing system for the first time. Secondly, the creation of Hangeul indicates that the history of human writing systems had shifted from the stage of phonemic writing to the stage of "featural writing system." That is, people have gone beyond phonemic writing systems like the Roman and Cyrillic alphabets to featural writing systems such as Hangeul. Finally, the book *Hunmin jeongeum* is the only record in the world that contains information on who made a certain script and how it was made. Therefore, the *Hunmin jeongeum* manuscript is a priceless treasure, unprecedented in human history, that records the principles of letter design.

Bibliography

An Byeong-hui. *Study on Korean Gugyeol of the Middle Ages (Jungse gugeo gugyeol ui yeongu)*. Iljisa, 1977.

Choe Hyeon-bae. *A Thesis on Hangeul (Hangeulgal)*. Jeongeumsa, 1942 · 1961.

Coulmas, Florian. *The Writing Systems of the World*. Basil Blackwell, 1989.

Daniels, P. T. & Bright, W. ed. *The World's Writing System*. Oxford University Press, 1996.

Gelb, I. J. *A Study of Writing*. The University of Chicago Press, 1952.

Hong Yun-pyo. *The Story of Hangeul 1 (Hangeul iyagi 1)*. Taehaksa, 2013.

__________. *The Story of Hangeul 2 (Hangeul iyagi 2)*. Taehaksa, 2013.

Jeong Gwang. *Hangeul and the Phags-pa Script (Hangeul gwa paspa munja)*. Youkrack Publishing Co., 2012.

Kang Sin-hang. *Creation of the Hunmin jeongeum and History of Research (Hunmin jeongeum changje wa yeongusa)*. Gyeongjin Munhwasa, 2010.

Kim Min-su. *Korean Language Policy (Gugeo jeongchaengnon)*. Korea University Press, 1973.

Lee Gi-mun. *Historical Study on the Korean Orthography (Gugeo pyogibeop ui yeoksajeok yeongu)*. Seoul National University Press, 1963.

__________. *Study on Hunmong jahoe (Hunmong jahoe yeongu)*. Seoul National University Press, 1971.

Lee Hui-seung. "The Story of Letters," *Hangeul 5 · 4*. 1937.

Lee Ik-seop. *Study on Korean Orthography (Gugeo pyogibeop yeongu)*. Seoul

National University Press, 1992.

Lee Ik-seop, Lee Sang-eok, Chae Wan. *The Korean Language (Hanguk ui eoneo).* Shingu Munhwasa, 1997.

Lee Sung-nyeong. *Essay on the Orthographic System Used in the Silla Period (Silla sidae ui pyogibeop chegye e gwanhan siron). Seoul National University Collected Papers* 2. 1955.

Nam Pung-hyeon. *Study on Orthography of Borrowed Words (Chaja pyo-gibeop yeongu).* Dankook University Press, 1981.

Park Byeong-chae. *History of the Development of Korean Letters (Hanguk munja baldansa), History of Korean Culture Series Vol. 5.* 1967.

Park Chang-won. *Hunmin jeongeum.* Shingu Munhwasa, 2005

__________. *Hangeul Museum (Hangeul bangmulgwan).* Chaeckmoon, 2011.

Sampson, G. *Writing Systems.* Stanford University Press, 1985.

Song Cheol-ui. *Linguistic Theories and Transcription Methods of Ju Si-gyeong (Jusigyeong ui eoneoiron gwa pyogibeop).* Seoul National University Press, 2010.

Vachek, J. *Written Language.* Mouton, 1973.

Yu Chang-don. *Eonmunji juhae.* Shingu Munhwasa, 1958.

Index

Park Chang-won

Born in Goseong, Gyeongsangnam-do Province
Received Bachelor's, Master's and Doctor's degrees from Seoul National University
Taught at Kyungnam University and Inha University
Currently professor at Ewha Womans University
Served as Head of the Language Research Division at the National Institute of the Korean Language, Managing Director of the Foundation International Korean Language, Member of the Korean Language Review Committee of the Ministry of Culture, Sports and Tourism, Chairman of the Association of Korean Language and Culture Centers, Chairman of the Society of Korean Linguistics, and Co-President of the Federation of Korean Language and Literature Associations

Books

Study on Korean Consonants of the Middle Ages, 1996
Language and the Social Status of Women, 1999
Ancient Korean Phonemes 1, 2002
History of Research on Korean Phonemes, 2002
Language Theory and Analysis, 2002
Language of South and North Korea and Korean Language Education, 2003
Hunmin jeongeum, 2005
Comparison of Korean, English and Japanese Phonemes, 2006
Refining Korean and Globalization of the Language 1, 2009
The Hangeul Museum, 2011
Orthography and Pronunciation of Korean, 2012
Over 100 theses on phonology and applied Korean language studies

Cho Yoon-jung

Cho Yoon-jung grew up in Australia and studied architecture at the University of New South Wales in Sydney. She now lectures at the Graduate School of Translation and Interpretation, Ewha Womans University.

Han Mi-sun

Han Mi-sun is a professional translator and lecturer at the Graduate School of Translation and Interpretation of Ewha Woman University, where she received her Ph.D. in Translation Studies.

Ewha Womans University Press Special Series

The Spirit of Korean Cultural Roots

1. *A Brief History of Korea* by Shin Hyong Sik
2. *Norigae*: Splendor of the Korean Costume by Lee Kyung Ja
3. *Roofs and Lines*: A Study of Korean Architecture by Yim Seock Jae
4. *Windows and Doors*: A Study of Korean Architecture by Yim Seock Jae
5. *Stone, Walls and Paths*: A Study of Korean Architecture by Yim Seock Jae
6. *The Traditional Space*: A Study of Korean Architecture by Yim Seock Jae
7. *Floral Lattices, Columns and Pavilions*: A Study of Korean Architecture by Yim Seock Jae
8. *Korean Dance* by Kim Malborg
9. *The Poetic World of Classic Korean Women Writers* by Lee Hai-soon
10. *Korean Mask Dance* by Cho Dong-il
11. *The Traditional Education of Korea* by Choi Wan Gee
12. *Folk-religion*: The Customs in Korea by Choi Joon-sik
13. *Money*: Traditional Korean Society by Won Yu Han
14. *Pottery*: Korean Traditional Handicrafts by Rha Sunhwa
15. *The Traditional Ships of Korea* by Choi Wan Gee
16. *Korean Travel Literature* by Kim Tae Joon
17. *Markets*: Traditional Korean Society by Chung Seung-mo
18. *Dining Tables*: Korean Traditional Handicrafts by Pai Man Sill
19. *Interior Space and Furniture of Joseon Upper-class Houses* by Choi Sang-Hun
20. *Modes of Transportation*: Traditional Korean Society by Choi Woun Sik
21. *Buddhism*: Religion in Korea by Choi Joon-sik
22. *Astronomy*: Traditional Korean Science by Changbom Park
24. *Festive Occasions*: The Customs in Korea by Yoon Seo-seok
25. *Traditional Korean Villages* by Oh Hong-seok
26. *Classical Poetic Songs of Korea* by Kim Dae-haeng
27. *Traditional Korean Painting* by Hong Sun-pyo
28. *Kimchi*: Traditional Korean Food by Kim Sook-he
29. *Korean Genealogical Records* by Chung Seung-mo
30. *Hangeul: The Korean Alphabet* by Park Chang-won

Hangeul
The Korean Alphabet

Written by Park Chang-won
Translated by Cho Yoon-jung and Han Mi-sun
Copy-edited by Jonathan Yeo

First published 31 August 2015
by Ewha Womans University Press
52, Ewhayeodae-gil, Seodaemun-gu, Seoul, Korea 03760
Tel. : 82-2-3277-2965, 362-6076
Fax. : 82-2-312-4312
E-mail: press@ewha.ac.kr
Homepage: www.ewhapress.com
Designed by GNA Communications

Price: 15,000 won
ISBN 979-11-85909-68-4 04710
ISBN 978-89-7300-602-1(set)

Printed in Korea